Assuming the Mantle of Leadership

Assuming the Mantle of Leadership

*Real-Life Case Studies
in Higher Education*

Perry R. Rettig

ROWMAN & LITTLEFIELD
Lanham • Boulder • New York • London

Published by Rowman & Littlefield
A wholly owned subsidiary of
The Rowman & Littlefield Publishing Group, Inc.
4501 Forbes Boulevard, Suite 200, Lanham, Maryland 20706
https://rowman.com

Unit A, Whitacre Mews, 26-34 Stannary Street, London SE11 4AB, United Kingdom

Copyright © 2018 by Perry R. Rettig

All rights reserved. No part of this book may be reproduced in any form or by any electronic or mechanical means, including information storage and retrieval systems, without written permission from the publisher, except by a reviewer who may quote passages in a review.

British Library Cataloguing in Publication Information Available

Library of Congress Cataloging-in-Publication Data

Includes bibliographic references and index.
ISBN 978-1-4758-4022-3 (cloth : alk. paper)
ISBN 978-1-4758-4023-0 (pbk. : alk. paper)
ISBN 978-1-4758-4024-7 (electronic)

∞ ™ The paper used in this publication meets the minimum requirements of American National Standard for Information Sciences Permanence of Paper for Printed Library Materials, ANSI/NISO Z39.48-1992.

Printed in the United States of America

Assuming the Mantle of Leadership is dedicated to my two daughters, Lisa Rettig and Kelly Paulsen. They have both been critical to my thinking and to my inspiration in terms of making these essential ideals and concepts pragmatic to everyday life in our institutions. In other words, they have helped ground my thinking and have pushed me to make this book a reality. The depth of my gratitude cannot be adequately described. I love you both.

Contents

Preface ix

Introduction xi

  1 Landing the Job 1
  2 And So It Begins 13
  3 It Can Only Get Better, Right? 21
  4 No Two Days Look the Same 27
  5 Never a Dull Moment 31
  6 When It Rains, It Pours 41
  7 Mother Never Said It Was Going to Be Easy 47
  8 Can I Get a Do-Over? 51
  9 With a Renewed Sense of Optimism 61
10 Just Another Day at the Office 73
11 Now I've Seen Everything 81
12 You Can Run, But You Can't Hide 89
13 The End Is Near 93
14 Don't Count Your Eggs Before They're Hatched 95

References 101

Index of Cases, In-Baskets, and Professional Reflections 103

About the Author 109

Preface

Those individuals aspiring to hold the mantel of leadership at institutions of higher learning most often emerge from the realms of content specialties. They have earned acclaim in their scholarly fields, ranging from the sciences to the humanities, and from the professions to the arts. They likely have had some quasi-administrative experience, be it as a department chair or a program coordinator. And they have likely received encouragement from their peers and those from the administrative positions to which they aspire. Yet they likely have a dearth of experience and formal training in terms of the breadth and scope requisite in the formal ranks of higher education leadership.

Technical coursework in higher education law and ethics, budgeting and finance, principles of management, philosophical and historical foundations, program assessment, and statistical analysis are necessary and appropriate, but such training lacks the genuine experience crucial for the preparation of our college and university leaders. Case studies and in-basket activities provide a closer approximation to real life, and they do so in the safe environs of a classroom with the neophyte surrounded by fellow aspirants. Even so, these case studies and in-basket activities are often rather removed from the actual context and life of the learner.

This book marries the simulation of the case study and in-basket approaches with the real-life or actual context of the reader. It truly gives the best of both worlds, while at the same time exploring the individual's philosophical and foundational beliefs that are essential to the higher education leader.

Introduction

This book uses approximations to the reader's reality in both time and space. For example, the case studies are designed to be completed within the context of the reader's reality. In other words, the student is asked to consider the case study as actually happening to them within their own institution, using their own policies and practices. In fact, the student is encouraged to consult with a mentor to see how that person would respond and why. Discussing cases and policies with a practicing mentor will have tremendous benefit to the preservice leader.

Further, students invariably find great benefit in discussing cases and in-basket activities with peers. In this manner, they can witness other institutions' policies and other individual students' approaches to difficult situations. The cases and in-baskets are purposefully not elaborate. This allows flexibility to each scenario to allow the student's own actual institutional context to provide the necessary elaboration.

The in-basket activities, on the other hand, are designed to take place instantaneously. In other words, the reader does not have the luxury of time, policy review, or consultation. Rather, the student is expected to respond in writing to each in-basket immediately, as they would in actual circumstances within the context of their own institution. Further, the student will have a series of in-basket activities to accomplish within a specified time period.

Finally, leaders need to be grounded in a strong philosophical foundation of guiding principles about their own role as leaders. With that said, this book provides a series of philosophical reflection opportunities within the text for the reader to consider the critical issues for aspiring leaders today, and to codify in writing their ideals.

It is suggested that in anticipation of these activities, the reader take a good amount of time to reflect on a series of foundational questions. These questions are designed to help elicit the reader's values and core beliefs about the people they hope to lead, about their own leadership style, and about how they should put into practice those fundamental beliefs and values.

All too often, without such reflection, people beginning in positions of authority and power do what they have seen done by their own previous administrators. This mimetic isomorphism promulgates the status quo of organizational leadership, and never takes into account what ought to be done and how. In other words, we manage and lead how we saw others manage and lead. We don't start by reflecting on what we believe about ourselves, about others, and how we should lead. To be more succinct, the reader is asked to examine their leadership presuppositions and to articulate their philosophy of leadership.

When approaching these cases, you might find it beneficial to think about the following questions: What is the relevant information? What other information is still needed or desired? Whom should I contact for this information or for advice? Who else is necessary to involve in the decision? What will be my approach to making the decision? What are my options? What is my choice and why?

An index of case studies and in-basket activities is included for your convenience and as a quick reference. The index lists each task chronologically as In-Basket (IB), Case Study (CS), or Philosophical Reflection (PR). Some tasks are listed as both In-Baskets and Case Studies. Further, each task is listed with such descriptors as: Policy or Communication or Planning, and whether it focuses more on faculty, staff, students, or external populations.

FOUNDATIONAL QUESTIONS IN PREPARATION FOR THE ACTIVITIES AHEAD

The reader is now encouraged to spend some time reading and reflecting upon several key aspects critical to higher education administrators. Part of this process is an opportunity to codify in writing their thoughts prior to engaging in the actual case study and in-basket activities. Being aware of one's own beliefs will be essential to making the decisions that lie ahead.

Shared Governance—Philosophical Foundation

Shared governance is the hallmark of the academe. Three anchors make up this troika of governing authority, and it is critical to understand the responsibilities of each. The tripartite anchors are the faculty, the administration, and the board of trustees or regents. In 1966 the American Association of University Professors issued what has become the seminal work explicating the roles of each body in its "Statement on Government of Colleges and Universities."

William Bowen and Eugene Tobin wrote a definitive book delineating the history of shared governance outlining the scope of authority of each anchor in *Locus of Authority: The Evolution of Faculty Roles in the Governance of Higher Education.*

The Association of Governing Boards' 2016 annual Association of Governance survey report indicated that only roughly 33 percent of college and university presidents felt that governing board members understand the work and responsibilities of faculty members well or very well. While there clearly are large areas of pragmatic overlap in some areas, there are certain areas that do reside in the domains of each body.

[Your task—Take a few moments to outline the key oversight responsibilities of faculty members, of administration, and of governing boards. Further, describe the purpose and necessity of shared governance.]

Motivation Theory—Philosophical Foundation

Douglas McGregor developed a model to help us characterize what we believe about human motivation. As a supervisor of employees, it is very important that you fully recognize your underlying assumptions about people. Once you are cognizant of your beliefs, you can then make appropriate and congruent decisions. McGregor explained that if you believe people are inherently lazy, self-centered, weak, selfishly competitive, or need to be externally motivated, then you are a proponent of Theory X.

On the other hand, Theory Y stipulates that people are inherently good, self-motivated, goal-oriented, cooperative, and hardworking. If people do show any characteristics of the negative behaviors associated with Theory X, it is because their work experiences have created conditions that foster this negativity.

[Your task—With that said, what do you believe about human nature? Are you more aligned with Theory X or Theory Y? Then, what does this mean to your leadership in terms of staff and faculty motivation, supervision and evaluation, decision-making, delegation, and committee leadership?]

Management and Leadership—Philosophical Foundation

Without a doubt, the position to which you aspire will require a varied mix of leadership and managerial attributes; often the line between the two is more blurred than pure theory would have us believe. Nonetheless, Professor John Kotter of the Harvard University School of Business clearly elucidated the distinctions between managers and leaders:

Managers	Leaders
Status Quo	Change
Planning and Budgeting	Setting Direction
Organizing and Staffing	Aligning People
Controlling/Problem-Solving	Motivating and Inspiring
Deductive	Inductive

[Your task—Do you agree with Kotter's attributes between the two? What changes or additions would you make? More importantly, what responsibilities of your new job will be more managerial in scope, and which will be more leadership-oriented? For example, will you be responsible for supervision and evaluation of staff, budgeting, assessment, program development, communication with various constituents, chairing committees, or any other tasks? And do you see each of these as managerial or leader-oriented? Take a few moments to write down your thoughts on these matters. As you progress through this book, keep these thoughts in mind.]

Leadership Style—Philosophical Foundation

Every leader will have a natural or inclined style of leadership—one that is suited to their own personality. It is important for the leader to understand this inclination and its inherent strengths and weaknesses. Dan Goleman (2000) explicated six leadership styles: coercive, authoritative, affiliative, democratic, pacesetting, and coaching. *Coercive* leaders demand immediate compliance, while *authoritative* leaders mobilize people. *Affiliative* leaders create harmony and build emotional bonds, while *democratic* leaders forge consensus through participation. Finally, *pacesetting* leaders set high standards for performance, while *coaching* leaders develop people for the future.

Most likely your own leadership style will depend upon the complexity of a given task and its context. Hersey and Blanchard (1988) created the Situational Leadership Model to describe attributes of leaders given the intricacies of certain circumstances. Here, each unique situation is a blend between a needed emphasis on task and on relationships. The first style is *autocratic directive*, where the emphasis is high on task focus and low on relationships. The *democratic collaborative* style emphasizes both high task and high relationship.

Encouraging nondirective leaders have a low focus on task and a high focus on relationships. Finally, *laissez-faire* leaders have a low emphasis on both task and relationships. The idea behind situational leadership is that the leader identifies both the ability and the willingness of employees to accomplish the task at hand. She or he then uses the style most appropriate to the given situation.

[Your task—While there are numerous ways to look at leadership styles, it is critical that you take some time to reflect on your preferred style. What style comes most naturally to you and is the approach that you will likely most often use? Are there times when this style is not appropriate? Take the time now to reflect on these questions. You may want to consider the leadership styles needed for chairing a committee, dealing with recalcitrant employees, supervising stellar employees, or leading a new initiative.]

Conflict Management—Philosophical Foundation

On a daily basis you will be challenged as you carry out your leadership agenda. Managing conflict will be critical to your work. There are numerous ways to handle conflict; each of us has a preferred way to handle these situations. It is critical for leaders to identify their own preferred method, so that when a situation arises they will understand whether their response is the most appropriate method or simply their inclined approach. There are times when one approach would be better than it would be at other times.

When your leadership is challenged, you may choose to *avoid* the problem, you may choose to *compromise*, or you may choose to *compete* in a win-lose approach. Likewise, you may also choose to make *accommodations* or to be *collaborative*.

[Your task—Please spend some time describing these five different ways of dealing with conflict. Then explain situations in which each one might be appropriate to use, as well as any problems that could be associated with that approach. For example, are there times when avoiding conflict is good, and are there times when it creates more problems? Finally, spend a few moments considering the one approach that you typically use. In other words, do you normally avoid conflict or do you find yourself using a competitive approach? Knowing the answer, what will this mean to how you deal with conflict in the future?]

Chapter One

Landing the Job

Dr. Leslie O'Connor began her career in the academy at a public state university as an assistant professor of Renaissance literature. She toiled in the ranks, teaching general education courses, advising undergraduates, publishing professional journal articles, presenting her research to national and international audiences, and serving on various college and university committees, until she was eventually promoted to associate professor.

She came directly out of her doctoral studies from a small private liberal arts college in the Deep South, but she was unsure where her career would take her. She really had no research focus when she entered her first job in higher education, but she hoped to help the next generation of students enjoy college as much as she had enjoyed it herself.

After being promoted to associate professor, Leslie reluctantly accepted her colleague's urging to chair the department. "Two years is all I'll give you," she promised. Leslie had found her scholarly focus and did not want to lose it. At the same time, she began to experience a sense of professional relevance as she began her three-year term on the faculty senate.

By the time she was up for tenure, Leslie knew she was prepared. She had, for the most part, strong support from her department colleagues, as well as those throughout the university. She enjoyed strong student surveys of her teaching, and she had become a fairly renowned scholar of Montaigne, having written over a dozen Tier I articles and two edited book chapters on the subject. In addition, she had presented her papers at over ten national and international professional conferences. She earned her tenure and promotion to full professor without any difficulties.

The first eight years of Leslie's academic career were not without trials and tribulations, but they seemed to fly by all the same. One month before the start of her ninth year, she was asked to serve as the interim associate dean of her college following the unexpected departure of the most recent associate. She was flattered but a little unnerved by not knowing the scope of her new responsibilities. Serving as department chair over the past several years had certainly helped to prepare her for these expanded duties, enough so that she applied for and was named the next dean of the college upon the retirement of her predecessor the following summer. It was a position she maintained for the next four years.

While her work as the department chair prepared her fairly well for the demands of the associate dean position, the latter had not prepared her for the scope and level of responsibilities of the position of academic dean. Budgeting, program assessment, and program development in academic areas outside her division challenged her early on. Promotion and tenure decisions, while a rewarding aspect of her job, were also very difficult. She made some tough decisions—decisions that might have cost her some friendships, or at least strained them.

At the same time, Leslie felt she had the respect of administrators across the campus. She was known for her hard work, her fairness in decision-making, and her compassionate leadership style. Leslie truly felt she was making a difference; she was ready for more. She applied to serve as the associate provost at her alma mater, and she was both excited and scared when she learned she would have an on-campus interview in two weeks. The phone interview had gone well for the most part. She did stumble in her response to describing key issues when contrasting conditions specific to public and private institutions. But the concerns regarding her answer to that question must not have been bad enough to keep her from moving to the next stage.

PREPARING FOR THE INTERVIEW

[Your task—Review the position announcement for Associate Provost at Gulf Vista University. Begin to outline your experiences and ideas for each of the key job responsibilities listed, and then draft a letter of application. Further, create a leadership profile or philosophy statement. Finally, review the interview agenda and delineate the key items you wish to cover for each portion of the interview.]

Associate Provost
Gulf Vista University
Position Announcement

Key Responsibilities

Supervise: Enrollment Management, Student Affairs, College Honors Program, Undergraduate Admissions, Graduate Admissions, Financial Aid.
Review renewal/promotion/tenure files.
Adjudicate student academic and grade appeals.
Serve as administrative representative to faculty senate and staff senate.

Qualifications

Earned doctorate.
Experience in leadership at an institution of higher education, preferably at the dean level or higher. Five years of increasing responsibility is preferred.
Experience with program development & assessment and regional or professional accreditation.

Interview Agenda

8:00–8:45 Breakfast at hotel with Dean of Arts and Sciences Dr. Benzar Hakeem
9:00–10:00 Tour of campus with two student ambassadors: TBD
10:00–10:45 Meeting with direct reports to the provost: Instructional Technology, Registrar, Financial Aid, Study Abroad, Enrollment Management, Undergraduate and Graduate Admissions, Tutoring Services, Student Affairs, Career Services, Residence Life, Counseling Services
10:45–11:00 Break
11:00–12:00 Open forum for faculty
12:00–1:00 Lunch with deans: Arts & Sciences; Business; Education and Human Services; Nursing and Allied Health Sciences; Graduate Programs; Library
1:15–1:45 Meeting with Human Resources
1:45–2:00 Break
2:00–3:00 Meeting with Search Committee
3:00–4:00 Meeting with student government representatives
4:00–5:00 Meeting with Provost and Vice President for Academic Affairs Dr. Ben Troulovetz

Chapter 1

THE INTERVIEW—YOUR LETTER OF APPLICATION

THE INTERVIEW—YOUR LEADERSHIP PROFILE OR PHILOSOPHY STATEMENT

THE INTERVIEW—IN-BASKET

[This first in-basket activity is actually a series of responses to questions Leslie was asked throughout the interview. Actually take the time to answer each question aloud as you would during an actual interview. You won't have notes to assist you, and you need to keep in mind how much time you would actually have in a real-life in-person interview.]

BREAKFAST INTERVIEW

7:55 a.m. Hoping to get to the lobby ahead of her breakfast companion, Leslie arrives a few minutes early. Dr. Hakeem is already there. He walks directly up to her, confidently shakes her hand, and makes her feel welcome. He looks Leslie straight in the eye during his entire introductory comments. Leslie walks to the hotel dining room, places her order with the waiter, and begins a casual conversation after a quick visit to the buffet.

Dr. Hakeem begins, "So, what brings you to Gulf Vista University, Dr. O'Connor?" Dr. Hakeem was a professor of mathematics when Leslie had attended GVU, but she had never been one of his students.

[Your Response]

After some brief small talk about her trip to Gulf Vista, Dr. Hakeem continues, "Why would you want to leave a tenured position earning a state pension and return to a private university, which lives by student enrollments?"

[Your Response]

He continues, "That's good; I'm just not sure I could do that. In any case, what does your family think about this possible move?"

[Your Response]

Finally, Dr. Hakeem apologetically states, "I'm sorry, I shouldn't have pried into your personal life. What do you like to do in your spare time?"

[Your Response]

"Before we go to the campus," Dr. Hakeem continues, "what are you most proud of at your present location? What's your greatest accomplishment?"

[Your Response]

"Good, good, good," Dr. Hakeem exclaims. "What initiatives or new programs would you like to make happen at Gulf Vista?"

[Your Response]

It is now 8:50, and Dr. Hakeem walks Leslie out to his personal car. He begins, "I won't be able to join you for lunch today, so I want to give you the chance to ask me any further questions you might have while we drive to your next stop. So please, fire away."

[Your Questions]

CAMPUS TOUR

Leslie's tour of the campus was scheduled to begin at 9:00, but they arrive at 9:10. The two student ambassadors are there waiting for her. They introduce themselves as Neisha Jones and Kyle Crandall. They seem rather shy and reluctant to talk. They ask Leslie what she'd like to see.

[Your Response]

You also use this opportunity to ask them questions over the next forty-five minutes.

[Your Questions]

MEETING WITH DIRECT REPORTS

It is now 10:05, and Leslie notices she is five minutes late for her meeting with her direct reports. The students escort Leslie to the conference room door and she walks in. The entire group is already seated; there is one seat open at the head of the conference room table. Victoria Suarez stands up, extends her hand, and introduces herself as the campus registrar. She motions Leslie over to the "hot seat."

Ms. Suarez makes welcoming comments and then asks each person around the room to introduce themselves, sharing both their position and how long they have worked at GVU. She then begins with her first question.

"Dr. O'Connor, what interests you about this position?"

[Your Response]

Director of Financial Aid Kimberly Grasse sits to the immediate right of Victoria Suarez and asks the next question. "What is the student loan default rate of your current school, and have you done anything to improve it? Also, we have a very large Pell Grant student body. How does that compare to your university? And do you have any special support for Pell-eligible students?"

[Your Response]

Mr. Ken Verkesne, director of instructional technology, follows: "Ms. O'Connor, what is your instructional technology platform, and are you comfortable with it? What are its perceived strengths and weaknesses?"

[Your Response]

Mr. Verkesne quickly interjects, "If I might follow up, what is your philosophy concerning online courses, and how do you ensure that faculty members are qualified to teach online?"

[Your Response]

Director of Undergraduate and Graduate Admissions Teresa Longstreet is next. "Hello, I'm so glad you have joined us today. I was very impressed with your letter of application. Can you tell us of any special attention or focus you give to recruiting nontraditional students, please? And, if I may as a follow-up, do you have any specific retention support in place particular to nontrads?"

[Your Response]

Dr. Eugene Golden is the director of enrollment management. He asks, "Can you describe your involvement in efforts to improve student retention in general? And what are your current retention rates?"

[Your Response]

Residence Life Director Michael Black is next. "Could you please tell us your philosophy for supervision of the residence halls? I'm referencing how strict you believe rules and adjudication should be."

[Your Response]

Finally, Ms. Farrah Fatallah, director of counseling services, concludes, "Dr. O'Connor, our time is almost up. While we didn't all get a chance to ask you questions, we want to give you the opportunity to ask us any questions you might have. We have a good five minutes left."

[Your Questions]

MEETING WITH FACULTY MEMBERS

With that, Leslie is escorted on to a large lecture hall in a neighboring academic building. Faculty Senate Chair Barbara Bouche serves as her escort and asks Dr. O'Connor if she would like to use the restroom.

After a brief restroom break, Leslie walks to the front of the auditorium. There are roughly one hundred faculty members in attendance. Dr. Bouche introduces Leslie by highlighting her résumé. She then asks Dr. O'Connor to begin by making some introductory remarks.

[Your Introductory Remarks]

A rotund, graying man stands up at the conclusion of Leslie's remarks. Without introducing himself, he asserts that higher education was founded on the principles of shared governance and faculty rights. He asks, "Professor O'Connor, what faculty rights do you espouse, and how will you practice the art of shared governance?"

[Your Response]

After Leslie's response, the gentleman walks out. Chair Bouche reminds those in attendance to introduce themselves to their guest before stating their questions.

A woman three rows back and to the right raises her hand. Chair Bouche calls on her. "Welcome, Dr. O'Connor. I'm Gena McCroy of the Music Department. We have heard rumors that senior administration is looking for ways to eliminate small departments, or departments that have larger overhead costs. How have you been able to mitigate these kinds of concerns at your current institution? Thank you."

[Your Response]

Professor McCroy is followed by a youthful-looking and bearded instructor. "Good morning. I'm Dennis Gabrielson. In two years I will be up for tenure if my esteemed and august colleagues are so willing." Chuckles rumble across the room. "When you examine tenure and promotion dossiers, precisely what are you looking for?"

[Your Response]

Leslie's response is followed by a motion from a tall and slender scholar standing in the back of the room. His sports jacket had been stylish back in the day, but it was worn by the years. "Good afternoon, ma'am. I'm Professor Harley Stevens. History Department. What do you see as the role of athletics in this academic institution? Thank you. I will now be seated and await your response."

[Your Response]

Chair Bouche makes a final comment. "We have time for one more query. Bea Gorges, can you bring us to closure?"

Dr. Gorges introduces herself as a professor of liberal studies. "We are finding that our incoming students aren't what they used to be. Their high school academic profiles are slipping, and quite frankly, they just aren't prepared for the rigors of college. Do you have any experience in preparing our youth for what is to be expected of them? And how can we balance the need for enrollment targets without lowering academic standards?"

[Your Response]

LUNCH WITH THE DEANS

With that, Dr. Bouche walks Leslie to the back of the auditorium, where Dean of the College of Business Ye Baong waits to take her to the student commons for lunch with the other deans. Dean Baong shows Leslie around the cafeteria and explains that she is free to choose from the wide variety of entrées and the like; then she is to join him and his colleagues in the glass-partitioned dining room across the way. Leslie collects her meal, walks into the dining room, sets down her tray, and goes around the room introducing herself to each of the deans.

The lunch begins with plenty of small talk, such questions as, "What do you like to read?" and "What do you do in your free time?" are asked.

After about ten minutes of this small talk, Dean Riley of the College of Education and Human Services jumps in. "Dr. O'Connor, how would you plan to go about evaluating your deans?"

[Your Response]

Library Dean Taylor follows with, "I appreciate your response, Dr. O'Connor. Could you tell us what budget model you would plan to use? And are you familiar with RCM, or Responsibility-Centered Management?"

[Your Response]

Dr. Albertine, the dean of nursing and allied health services, raises her hand. "Dr. O'Connor, what do you see as your role, and the dean's role, in faculty renewal, promotion, and tenure decisions? Also, have you ever overturned a dean's decision?"

[Your Response]

"Hello, Dr. O'Connor. I'm Henry Kyle, dean of graduate studies. You've obviously had the opportunity to research us a bit on our website, and of course, you've already met a number of our colleagues. What, if anything, strikes you the most about Gulf Vista University? What new initiatives would you work on?"

[Your Response]

"If I may, I would like to follow up on your response, Dr. O'Connor. I'm Dr. Korschvitz, dean of students. What would your first one hundred days in office look like?"

[Your Response]

Dean of the College of Business Dr. Ye Baong pulls the conversation to a close. "Leslie, you've barely had a chance to eat any lunch. Why don't you ask us any questions you have, and while we're answering you can eat."

[Your Questions]

Dr. Baong and his colleagues stand up to shake Leslie's hand and thank her for joining them for lunch. Dr. Baong then escorts Leslie to the office of human resources.

MEETING WITH HUMAN RESOURCES

Ms. Becca Sorenson, the director of HR, is on her phone, but she waves Leslie into her office and motions for her to sit in a chair across from her desk. Leslie can surmise that she is talking to an attorney representing the university in a personnel dispute. Leslie feels a bit awkward and uncomfortable as Ms. Sorenson mentions several employees' names. The telephone conversation goes on for nearly five minutes, but it seems like an eternity before the HR director hangs up the phone.

"Good afternoon, Dr. O'Connor. I'm sorry for keeping you waiting—just another day at the office. I'm Becca. Here, I have some benefits documents for you that we share with all prospective employees. I can assure you that we have a very fair benefits package. Rather than reading this to you, why don't I just let you ask me any questions you have."

[Your Questions]

At the conclusion of this brief appointment in Human Resources, Ms. Sorenson asks her administrative assistant to walk Dr. O'Connor to her next scheduled appointment. Leslie is scheduled for a break at this time as well, so she arrives at the conference room in the library twenty minutes early. She is left alone and feeling a bit numb from the whirlwind activities of the day. She spends this time gathering her thoughts. Soon thereafter the search committee members begin to trickle in.

SEARCH COMMITTEE

[What small talk do you initiate with these people as they enter?]

Once the committee members are all assembled, the next round of interviews begins. Dr. Sally Taylor—dean of the library—whom Leslie met earlier is the first to speak up. "As chair of the search committee, I want to welcome you to Gulf Vista University. I trust you have been treated well today, but I also know you must be exhausted. Let's start off with giving you the opportunity to introduce yourself and tell us what compelled you to want to join our family here at GVU."

[Your Response]

"Thank you, Dr. O'Connor. I'm SuYe Kim, coordinator for study abroad. I have a two-part question: Can you tell us a bit about your experiences with study-abroad programs? Then, can you tell us what ideas you have to increase student participation in study-abroad programming?"

[Your Response]

"Dr. O'Connor, I am pleased to meet you. I am Dr. Miles Crenshaw—director of assessment and accreditation liaison. A significant responsibility of the associate provost is the general oversight of assessment and accreditation. As a matter of fact, I report directly to the associate provost. Could you spend a few minutes sharing with us your experiences and background in the areas of assessment and accreditation?"

[Your Response]

"I'd like to follow up if I may," continues Dr. Crenshaw. "Can you give an example of a time when you had to move any recalcitrant faculty members who did not want to change? Then, if you could follow up by telling me and the committee how you would motivate academic departments that are dragging their heels in completing their assessment responsibilities? Thank you."

[Your Response]

Athletic Director Pete Flattery is next. "Dr. O'Connor, we have an expanding divide between faculty and coaches on this campus. Many coaches complain that faculty members don't communicate with them about their student athletes. What I'm trying to say is that we know our kids better than anyone else on campus, and we can be a huge help. We just need the faculty to tell us when a kid isn't coming to class or making satisfactory progress. How has your relationship with your coaches been? And how can you help us bridge this gap?"

[Your Response]

"Dr. O'Connor, please let me introduce myself. I'm Mary Rice. I'm the provost and vice president's administrative assistant, and I am also the staff representative on this committee. I work for both the provost and his associate. Do you have any thoughts about the role of staff in decision-making? In particular, our staff council is concerned that we're not currently treated as equals in this regard. I'm not saying we feel like second-class citizens, but is there anything you would do to improve the climate for our staff?"

[Your Response]

"Good afternoon, Dr. O'Connor. I'm Jerome May, and I am serving as the alumni rep on this committee. We are delighted to have you visit with us today. I've been very impressed with your credentials. What has been your experience in utilizing the wealth of human resources among alumni?"

[Your Response]

As Leslie is wrapping up her comments, a student walks into the room. "Oops, I'm early." He quickly scoots back out and closes the door.

Dr. Taylor laughs and states, "Well, that is as good a segue as any. Before we conclude, Dr. O'Connor, do you have any final comments or questions for the search committee?"

[Your Questions]

STUDENT GOVERNMENT

The committee members leave the room, and six students take their place. Leslie is about to meet with the Student Government Association. Dr. Taylor stays with the group. She makes some welcoming comments, then asks each student to introduce themselves, stating both their year and their major. She then turns the session over to the SGA president.

"Good afternoon, Dr. O'Connor." SGA President Xena Washington starts with the first question. "As you know, we have a traditional SGA. We're an active group, and we get along quite well. However, some students are asking if we could start a black student union group. What are your thoughts on that topic?"

[Your Response]

"Ms. O'Connor, please allow me to introduce myself. I am Herbert Walker. While I'm vice president of the SGA, I am also a military veteran. Without making it a big deal, I conducted an informal survey of vets on campus. We feel that some of the administrative offices on campus, in particular Financial Aid and the registrar's office, could do a better job of communicating with us. Well, it's actually more than that. We don't think we're always listened to or treated with the respect we deserve. Would you provide any sensitivity training on this issue for your staff?"

[Your Response]

Graduate student Melanie Henderson follows. "Dr. O'Connor, I just graduated with a bachelor's degree in business this past May and have just started my MBA. I have been a nontraditional student. Is there anything you have done to make nontraditional students and commuting students feel more a part of the campus? Also, we would like to be offered weekend courses, but our college has made it a point not to teach on weekends. Would you allow some weekend course offerings?"

[Your Response]

Willa Probst asks, "Dr. O'Connor, most students are concerned that the student evaluation surveys they complete at the end of the semester are meaningless. We don't think the professors or the administrators even look at them. How have you used these student survey results to improve instruction or eliminate poorly performing professors?"

[Your Response]

Dean Taylor interjects, "We're about out of time. Gabriel, you've been sitting there quietly. What would you like to ask Dr. O'Connor?"

"Sure. Dr. O'Connor, why do you want to leave the classroom and become an administrator?"

[Your Response]

Gabriel then walks Leslie to her final appointment of the day—to meet with Provost/VPAA Dr. Ben Troulovetz. Because she didn't get the opportunity to ask the students any questions of her own, she uses her walk with Gabriel to ask several questions.

[Your Questions]

MEETING WITH PROVOST/VICE PRESIDENT FOR ACADEMIC AFFAIRS

It is 4:00 on the dot. Dr. Troulovetz is walking down the hall toward Leslie from the other direction. He grips her hand firmly and asks, "Have you survived?"

[Your Response]

He continues, "Leslie, we've talked on the phone earlier. You've answered other people's questions all day. Now it's your turn."

[Your Response/Questions]

The conversation goes on for about half an hour. Then Dr. Troulovetz gets up and walks to the door. Before he opens the door to the outer suite, he states, "We've got another couple of finalists. The committee should get back to me by the end of next week, and then someone will get back to you after that. I hope you have a safe trip home. It's truly been a pleasure to have you on our beautiful campus."

THE OFFER

Leslie eventually received a phone call from Provost Troulovetz himself. "Leslie, how are you doing?" Not waiting for her response, he went on, "I've got some great news for you. We'd like to bring you on board. How does that sound?"

Leslie responded enthusiastically but with appropriate opprobrium.

The provost continued, "Well, I'm delighted. Say, we'd like to offer you a competitive salary. And I want to add that we give all junior administrators one-year contracts."

Leslie was concerned about receiving only a one-year contract, and she stumbled a moment when she heard the salary that was being offered. She was hoping for at least $10,000 more annually, and she didn't know what to think about the one-year offer.

[Your Response]

Chapter Two

And So It Begins

Leslie has accepted the position at Gulf Vista University and she arrives for her first day of work. Eager to get started, Leslie arrives before her office staff. She sits behind her desk, logs on to her computer, and begins reading her email. Quickly she sees that many outside vendors have great ideas of ways to improve her organization, from webinars to conferences and from technology innovations to Title IX mandatory compliance training. For the time being, she skips these advertisements and finds the emails directly written to her.

> *[Your task—Write a response to each person, in order. At the same time, write down a list of things you need to do later, the people with whom you will speak, and the policies you will need to explore. This will become your next case study. You have thirty minutes in total to answer these five in-basket emails.]*

IN-BASKET

(IB 1) EMAIL 1 — COMFORT DOG — [POLICY — STUDENTS]

Ms. O'Connor,
    I am a new student on campus this year. I need to have my comfort dog with me at all times. I was told I should tell you, just a heads-up.
    Thank you, Kylie Aisha

[Your Response and Task List]

(IB 2) EMAIL 2—VACATION REQUEST—[POLICY—STAFF]

Dear Dr. O'Connor~

Welcome to GVU. I hate for this to be my first formal interaction with you, but I am requesting to take this Thursday and Friday off from work. My best friend from college is getting married this weekend, and I am flying to Lake Tahoe. I've already purchased the plane tickets. I hope this is not a problem.

In advance, thank you. Ken Verkesne

[Your Response and Task List]

(IB 3) EMAIL 3—FAMILY ON STUDY AWAY—[POLICY—FACULTY/STAFF]

Hello, Leslie:

I want to run this idea past you early. Dr. Sesler (associate professor of art history) will be leading a J-Term trip to Eastern Europe. He would like to take his son Kyle along. Kyle will be a first-semester freshman starting this coming spring. Will you permit him to go on the trip? We have two prohibitions that need to be considered. First, we typically do not allow family members to travel on these trips. Second, we do not permit students who haven't taken classes yet to go on these trips. I would like to support this request, but I do understand it could be a slippery slope. Thank you for your consideration. SuYe

[Your Response and Task List]

(IB 4) EMAIL 4—CONFIDENTIAL—[ETHICS]

Dear Dr. O'Connor,

I write this note to you in complete confidence. In other words, I would like this to remain between the two of us. Would you join me tomorrow morning for a cup of coffee at Bagley's Bagels shop on Seventh Avenue?

Regards,
Vic Torrington, Board of Trustee member

[Your Response and Task List]

(IB 5) EMAIL 5—BLACK STUDENT UNION—[POLICY—STUDENTS]

Good morning, Dr. O'Connor,

You may remember me from your interview. I'm the president of the SGA. A fairly good-sized group of African American students, myself in-

cluded, would like to begin our own black student union. We invite you to join us this Wednesday evening at 7:30 p.m. in the Common Area of Woodruff Hall. This will give you an opportunity to hear our thoughts and concerns, and at the same time we could listen to your ideas.
Most appreciatively,
Xena Washington, SGA president

[Your Response and Task List]

(CS 1) CASE STUDY—IN-DEPTH REVIEW

Review in greater depth your task lists from each of the five emails above. With whom would you like to speak besides the email writer? What are the pertinent policies and practices at your own institution? How will they guide your decision-making? What latitude do you have, if any? Would you change any of your initial email responses or decisions?

(CS 2) CASE STUDY—STRATEGIC PLANNING—[PLANNING]

Dr. Troulovetz steps into Leslie's office and asks to chat for a few minutes. He begins, "Leslie, I know you have had some experience with strategic planning. I'd like for you to lead the division of Academic Affairs in strategic planning this year. I estimate that your task will take the entire academic year and culminate in approval by the full Board of Trustees during our summer retreat."

Leslie sat wide-eyed for a moment. She had participated in strategic planning efforts at the school level earlier, but she had never led such a large endeavor. The most she'd ever done was to chair a subcommittee. Still, she knew this was a tremendous opportunity to show her leadership skills, so she replied, "I'd be delighted to lead this project, Ben. Before I begin, do you have a charge for the group? And, speaking of the group, who do you have in mind to join? Will you be on it yourself?"

"Well, I won't be on the planning team, Leslie. The team will ultimately report to me. I would like for you to draft a charge memo that I will send to you and the team. So, please put together a draft charge, along with a list of potential team members. You don't have to put every individual's name down, but put down any positions or representations the best you can. We can discuss the team once your draft is done. Also, please put together a drafted timeline for me. Let's discuss all of this when we meet next week."

"Very good, Ben. This sounds like fun," came Leslie's somewhat stunned response.

Ben cast a perplexed look her way. "'Fun'? Well, we'll see about that."

[Your case assignment is to draft a charge memo for strategic planning in the division of Academic Affairs. In addition, put together a list of potential team members, as well as a potential timeline for the work to be accomplished.]

IN-BASKET

(IB 6) PHONE CALL—STUDENT NEWSPAPER— [COMMUNICATION]

After Dr. Troulovetz left Leslie's office, her administrative assistant, Mary Rice, walked in. "Dr. O'Connor, while you were meeting with Provost Troulovetz, Aminah Busra called. She would like for you to call her back."

Leslie squinted quizzically. "Who is Aminah?"

"Oh, I'm sorry. Aminah is the editor of the student newspaper, *The Leagues*. I'm sure she wants to interview you for her next issue."

[Your task is to list the questions you have for the phone call and the points you want to make certain you cover ahead of time.]

(IB 7) WALK-IN VISITOR—FACULTY SENATE— [COMMUNICATION]

As Leslie hung up the phone, there was a knock on the door. It was Mary Rice, again, but standing immediately behind her was Barbara Bouche—the faculty senate chair. "Dr. O'Connor, do you have two minutes for Dr. Bouche?" she asked.

Leslie nodded. "Of course. Come on in, Barbara."

"I know how busy you are, Leslie, but the faculty senate is requesting that you attend our first senate meeting of the year. We would like to welcome you and have you share your plans for the upcoming year."

Leslie's mind was racing. What would she want to say? "I'd be happy to be your guest. Let's discuss the points I should cover."

[Your task is to put together a quick list of the several key points you would want to prepare for the faculty senate meeting. You have three minutes to do this.]

(IB 8) STUDY AWAY—CHANGE IN PLANS—[POLICY]

Leslie decided to take a walk around the academic quad to clear her head. This might not have been a good idea. Within moments of stepping outside, she was stopped by a young faculty member who spoke with great quickness and intense focus.

"Good morning, Dr. O'Connor. I'm Cindy Vaughan, assistant professor of history. I have a question. SuYe said I should ask you."

Barely able to catch her breath, Leslie replied, "It's a pleasure to meet you, Dr. Vaughan. Can you remind me who SuYe is?"

"Oh, yes. She is the coordinator for study-away programs. I will be taking two dozen students to Scotland this summer. Because of family health issues, my co-instructor will no longer be able to go with us. But I have a great solution. My fiancé, Michael, could join us. He is a public school history teacher. SuYe said I should ask you if this would be alright."

> *[Your task is to elicit some answers from Cindy to questions that you might have before you make a decision or at least before you meet with SuYe. You have three minutes to complete this task.]*

Leslie short-circuited her walk around the quad and headed back to her office. Just as she sat back down behind her desk, the phone rang. The caller ID showed that it was Martin Gregory. But who was that?

(IB 9) PHONE CALL—COLLABORATIVE PARTNERSHIP— [COMMUNICATION—EXTERNAL]

Leslie picked up the phone. "Hello, this is Dr. Leslie O'Connor."

"Welcome aboard, Leslie," came the enthusiastic reply. "I'm Martin Gregory, your counterpart at Tri-County Community College. Please call me Marty."

"Good morning, Marty. It's a pleasure to meet you, so to speak," said Leslie. "What can I do for you?"

"Well, most likely you don't know about it yet, but TC3 has an excellent emergency management officer training program. It's been very successful, and dozens and dozens of our alumni serve as active officers in the tri-county region. The program has been so successful that we are now being asked by county agencies to start a management program for officers who wish to become captains and chiefs. This would be an excellent opportunity for both of our schools to cooperate and serve a growing niche. What do you think?"

"That sounds like an intriguing idea, Marty. I do have a couple of questions before we go down this road, however."

> *[Your task is to quickly prepare some questions you would have for Dr. Gregory. You have three minutes to complete this task.]*

(IB 10) MEETING—ENROLLMENT MANAGEMENT—[COMMUNICATION]

No sooner had Leslie hung up the phone than in walked Dr. Eugene Golden, the director of enrollment management. He began, "If we leave now, we'll only be a couple of minutes late for the meeting."

Leslie was perplexed. "What meeting?"

"The EMT meeting. I'm sure it's on your calendar, Les. We co-chair the biweekly EMT meeting. Isn't it on your calendar?"

Leslie didn't even take the time to look. She grabbed her notepad and headed out the door with Dr. Golden. "On our way, I've got some questions," Leslie stated.

> *[Your task is to ask the questions you would like answers to before you walk into the meeting. You have three minutes to do this.]*

(CS 3) CASE STUDY—IN-DEPTH REVIEW

You didn't get a chance to go into any depth on the above in-basket activities. Examine your own institution's policies and guidelines. Take the time to frame out coherent decisions for each in-basket. Please do feel free to seek guidance from colleagues and mentors as you prepare these responses, but limit them to one page each.

(CS 4) CASE STUDY—PAY FOR PLAY?—[NCAA]

Leslie opened her mail and found an unsigned, typed-out letter. It read:

> Dr. O'Connor:
> I have learned that some of our student athletes are receiving "paid internships" or "leadership scholarships," in clear violation of NCAA Division III policy. In none of these cases are the athletes actually doing internships or conducting leadership activities. This must be reported and rectified immediately. Doing so promptly may limit our punishment by the NCAA.
> Regards,
> Concerned Faculty Member

> *[Your response—Whom do you contact? What are the questions you seek to answer? Is this indeed an NCAA violation for Division III universities? What about for Divisions I and II?]*

(CS 5) CASE STUDY—NEED FOR TENURE?—[FACULTY]

At home that evening, Leslie decided to open her email to see if anything pressing had come in since she had left the office. Mainly, she was looking to see if Provost Troulovetz had sent her anything. Indeed, he had sent an email at 5:35 p.m. It read:

> Hi, Leslie. I had hoped to catch you before you left for the day. In any case, it struck me today when talking to a couple of our trustees that they don't understand the rationale for faculty tenure. Further, I don't think the faculty roles in shared governance are apparent to our governing board. Could you jot down a few notes about rationale for tenure and faculty roles in shared governance? We can discuss this when we meet on Thursday morning.
>
> *[Your response—Spend some time putting together an outline providing historic rationale for faculty tenure and for faculty roles in shared governance. You could find help that is documented from the AAUP and AGB. Your faculty handbook and board bylaws would be excellent resources, as well.]*

Chapter Three

It Can Only Get Better, Right?

(CS 6) CASE STUDY—PRAYER REQUEST—
[POLICY—STUDENTS]

Leslie was hoping to arrive to her office before anyone else got there; she wanted some quiet time to prepare for the day. But as she rounded the corner to her office, she noticed a hulking young man standing outside her door.

"Excuse me, but are you Dr. O'Connor?" the young man began.

He seemed kind enough to Leslie. He put out his hand to shake hers. "Yes, I am," came Leslie's response.

"Good morning, ma'am. I'm Kyle Franklin. I'm one of the captains of the football team. Could I speak with you for a few moments?"

Leslie welcomed Kyle into her office. She noticed a tattoo of a cross on his hairy, bulging bicep. She smiled to herself—the image of a hairy cross seemed odd.

Kyle continued, "A group of us, from different teams, eventually want to petition the Campus Activities Board to start a chapter of the Fellowship of Christian Athletes. But that's not what I'm here about this morning. You see, we're coming up on the one-year anniversary of the death of our beloved football coach Gus Giovanni. We'd like to hold a prayer vigil in remembrance of Coach. We would like to open it to any students or faculty, and hold it on the quad this Friday evening at 9:00 p.m. Will you give us permission to do this?"

> *[Your response—What do you say to Kyle at the moment? Then, as a case study response, check to see if there are any policies that might help you address this question. Further, seek advice from several of your colleagues. What other things need to be considered?]*

(CS 7) CASE STUDY—MUSLIM SAFE PLACE— [POLICY—COMMUNICATION—STUDENTS]

Leslie read her next email. It was from student Aminah Busra.

> Re: Muslim Student Safe Place
> Dear Dr. O'Connor:
>   A number of our Muslim students have approached me with concerns about their safety and about some general harassment. I don't have any specific complaints to share, but many of us feel we're not being treated very well. In any case, it has been suggested that the campus secure a safe place for us to get together during the day for our prayers. We'd like it to be private, but in a decent location. Do you have any ideas? Also, when you have some time, I would like to meet with you and give you a copy of the Quran.
>   Thank you in advance,
>   Aminah
>
> *[Your response—Write an email response to Aminah. Before you do this, carefully consider your institution's policies, any concerns to address, and ideas you might have for Aminah.]*

(IB 11) IN-BASKET—UNDOCUMENTED STUDENTS— [POLICY—STUDENTS]

Leslie had just finished responding to Aminah when Mary Rice popped her head into the office. "Dr. O'Connor? Could you take this call? It's from an angry parent, and he is demanding that either you or the president talk with him."

Leslie didn't want to take the call, but she felt it was better for her to take it than have it sent to the president. "Sure, transfer the call on in."

"Hello, this is Dr. O'Connor," she answered when the phone buzzed.

"Yes, my name is Laura Donovan. I received word last week that my daughter Brittany was not accepted to your university because her test scores were too low. Then I found out that you are accepting undocumented students from Mexico. Is that true? I demand to know the truth, and I want my daughter accepted to your college!"

Leslie was, of course, taken aback by this verbal assault. She didn't know what to say, but she felt she needed to at least give some response. "Ma'am, I don't know any specifics about either your daughter's application or the undocumented students. Please allow me to look into this matter and return your call."

[Your response—Take a look at your institution's policies and procedures for admissions. Also, verify your institution's handling of DACA students. Then

prepare an outline of the issues you will address on a return phone call to Mrs. Donovan.]

(CS 8) CASE STUDY—ACTIVE SHOOTER: TABLETOP— [POLICY—COMMUNICATION]

Leslie returned to her email. After scrolling through the ever-increasing number of unread mail, she noticed an email from Provost Troulovetz. The subject line read: "Active Shooter Tabletop." This heading grabbed her attention. It was written to Campus Police Chief Timothy Smith; Dean of Students Dr. Helga Korschvitz; Director of Residence Life Mr. Michael Black; Vice President for Advancement, Marketing, and Communications Shirlee Reed; and Leslie. She read the body of the email.

> With the recent spate of gun violence in society and on college campuses, it is most prudent for us to reexamine our preparedness and response for an active shooter incident on campus. Therefore, I am pulling together an ad hoc committee to address this issue. You will each serve as university representatives on this team, and I will be bringing in representatives from the community. These individuals will include people from local law enforcement, the regional hospital, and the media.
>
> In order to prepare for this meeting, please review our current emergency plan, as well as those from a few aspirant institutions. Be ready to discuss improvements you would suggest to the plan. Our meeting will include the initial framing of a tabletop exercise to practice this summer. A calendar invitation and agenda will follow soon. In advance, I thank you for the work you will do in this most critical endeavor.
>
> *[Your response—Review your institution's emergency preparedness plan for an active shooter situation. Meet one on one with key individuals on your campus to learn how your campus would respond. What different aspects of the plan need to be considered and communicated?]*

(IB 12/CS 9) IN-BASKET AND CASE STUDY—PROPERTY RIGHTS—[COMMUNICATION—STUDENTS]

Mary Rice knocked on Leslie's office door, then walked in. "Excuse me, Dr. O'Connor, but a student is waiting outside. He says he won't leave until you speak with him. What should I say to him?"

Leslie paused. She thought, *Tell him to make an appointment*. But she immediately decided against that. "What does he want?"

Mary Rice told Leslie that Sebastian Morolokov was a music major. He had just discovered that his music locker had been broken into and his personal trumpet significantly vandalized. Sebastian wanted the school to find out who did this, and he wanted the school to pay for a new instrument.

[Your response—What questions do you have of Sebastian? With what other people would you want to speak? If, after investigating the case, it could not be determined who vandalized the instrument, should the school pay to replace it? If so, would the university's insurance cover the cost? If the institution does pay for it, which account would you use?]

(CS 10) CASE STUDY—DASHBOARDS—
[PLANNING—COMMUNICATION]

Leslie received another email from Ben. This particular email was written only to her. The subject heading read, "Dashboards."

Leslie, President Boggs has requested that each member of the leadership team create a virtual dashboard of analytics for their respective positions. Please investigate a list you would find beneficial. A good place to start, I would conjecture, would be with your counterparts at other similar institutions. We can talk about this at our next 1:1. As I am putting together my own list, I have been asking my direct reports, "What data do I constantly ask you for?" Those are quick ways of identifying dashboards. You might want to do the same.

Oh, I also have a special favor to ask. I'm on the Chamber of Commerce Planning Committee. I need to find guests for next month's luncheon. I'd like for you to speak, twenty minutes tops, about yourself and what kind of work you're doing for us here at Gulf Vista.

[Your response—Take the time to do just what Dr. Troulovetz requested. What analytical dashboard items would you like to use for the position in which you are pursuing? Talk with colleagues at work and at other institutions to find out what they use. Do you presently use any dashboards?]

(IB 13) IN-BASKET—ALCOHOL VIOLATION—
[POLICY—ETHICS—FACULTY]

Leslie decided she needed some fresh air, so she took a walk down to the mailroom. She saw the assistant women's basketball coach, Samantha Redmond, standing at the mailboxes with a blank stare on her face.

Leslie casually greeted Samantha. "How are you doing today, Coach?"

Samantha turned toward Leslie with a mixed look of surprise and confusion. "Oh, ah . . . fine."

Leslie had a sinking feeling. Samantha's eyes appeared somewhat glassy, and she wasn't sure, but it seemed like she smelled alcohol on Samantha's breath.

[Your response—What would you do in Leslie's situation—on the spot and in follow-up? You have three minutes to describe what you would do at this very moment. What would you say and do? Then later take the time to ask your mentor how to handle such a situation. What are your legal responsibilities? What would you need to document?]

(IB 14) IN-BASKET—ADMISSIONS TOURS— [COMMUNICATION—STUDENTS]

After the incident in the mailroom, Leslie truly felt the need to get some fresh air—both literally and figuratively—so she headed outside. As she walked toward the library, she saw a scene that put a smile on her face. One of the student ambassadors from the Admissions Office was giving a campus tour. Upon closer inspection, however, Leslie noticed that the young ambassador was wearing the customary campus polo, but it was untucked, his khaki pants were rumpled and stained, and it looked as if he had just gotten out of bed.

While that general appearance made Leslie feel uncomfortable, what the young ambassador said to the visiting student and his parents made her genuinely upset. The tour guide stated in a hushed and joking tone, "This is the library. It's the last time you'll see it—nobody ever goes there."

[Your response—Would you say anything to the ambassador or the family at this moment? Presently, write down the notes you plan to discuss with the director of the Admissions Office. What will be your expectations? Will you have a follow-up?]

(CS 11) CASE STUDY—FREEDOM OF SPEECH— [POLICY—COMMUNICATION]

Thinking things couldn't get any worse, Leslie decided to head back to her office via a circuitous route through the parking lot. While there, she noticed that each car had a half sheet of paper stuck under a windshield wiper. When she stopped at her own car, she pulled the sheet out, which read:

> Support your LGBT friends! Fund-raiser event tonight!
> Academic Quad at 7:15 p.m.
> Free Music
> Sponsored by Campus LGBT Council

Leslie had no concern about the event, but she didn't know the policy for putting flyers on people's cars. Certainly this was not permitted. She took the flyer back to the office.

26   *Chapter 3*

As she walked into her office, she handed Mary the flyer. "All the cars in the lot have these placed under their windshield wipers, Mary. What is our policy on such activities?"

"Oh, I'm sure that is against policy, but people still do it from time to time," came Mary's response.

Mary read the flyer to herself, then muttered loud enough for Leslie to hear, "This must be what caused that phone call."

"What phone call?" Leslie queried.

"Oh, Reverend Daniels from the church down the street called. He wants to hold a rally this evening by the library. He said he just was giving you a courtesy call to let you know."

> *[Your response—Review your institution's policies on the posting of flyers on cars parked on campus, and any requirements and permissions for external groups to hold free-speech rallies on campus property. Do you have any allotted locations for such activities? Is there a form that such groups need to complete? Who makes the decision? After reviewing your current policies, how would you respond to the LGBT Council and to Reverend Daniels?]*

(IB 15) IN-BASKET—STAFF MEETING AGENDA—[PLANNING]

After dinner that night, Leslie opened her laptop to review her schedule for the upcoming week. She noticed that her first full staff meeting was scheduled. She began typing up an agenda for this initial meeting so that she could distribute it first thing in the morning.

> *[Your response—Put together your first staff meeting agenda. What are the key points you wish to cover with your entire staff—to set the tone and philosophy of your administration? What do you want to accomplish in your first one hundred days?]*

Chapter Four

No Two Days Look the Same

(CS 12) CASE STUDY—NEW ACADEMIC PROGRAM—
[POLICY—ACADEMICS]

First thing the next morning, Leslie sent an email to her staff with the next week's council meeting agenda. Soon after, she received an email response from Dean Hakeem of the College of Arts and Sciences. It read:

Dr. O'Connor:
    Dr. Ye Baong of the College of Business and I have an item for the next Council meeting. We would like to propose a new academic major cross-listed between our two colleges. The major would be Technology Management. With your approval, we would like to discuss this topic with the other deans and directors.

[Your response—What are the issues you would like to have investigated and covered when exploring a new academic program? Do you have a form or a rubric to complete for new academic program proposals? Would you do a market analysis? Put together a list of questions and comments. Then formulate an email response to Drs. Baong and Hakeem.]

(IB 16) IN-BASKET—WALKABOUT—[COMMUNICATION]

Leslie really had wanted to visit the different offices that reported to her. She wanted to see where everyone worked and meet the support staff. She jotted down the names of the different offices and a couple of questions she wanted to ask of the staff in each. Moments later she was out the door.

[Your response—List the names of the different offices that would likely be reporting to you. What do you want to make certain you say to people, even if

only informally, as you visit them at their offices? What questions do you have of them?]

(IB 17) IN-BASKET—TRANSCRIPT HOLD—
[POLICY—STUDENTS]

The first stop Leslie made was at the Office of the Registrar. Victoria Suarez greeted Leslie, gave her a quick tour of the office, and introduced her to the staff.

Victoria then remarked, "Dr. O'Connor, your visit to our office this morning was fortuitous. We had a request from a former student who left us after his sophomore year. We have a financial hold on his transcripts because he has an unpaid bill of five hundred eighty-four dollars. He last attended here twelve years ago, and he now wants to complete his degree at another institution in another state. We have a standing practice not to release official transcripts with outstanding bills. I explained this to him, but he is asking us to waive this practice; he has only nine credits to take in order to graduate. What do you want us to do?"

[Your response—Do you support this practice? This individual cannot start at the next university, move on with his education/career aspirations, without an official transcript. What is your institution's policy? Is there a compromise that can be made? Or do such compromises lead to a slippery slope and possible unintended consequences?]

(IB 18) IN-BASKET—PARENT CONCERN/FERPA—
[EXTERNAL—COMMUNICATION (STUDENT/FACULTY)]

As she left the registrar's office, Leslie nearly bumped into a gentleman walking past the door. He didn't seem to know where he was going, so Leslie introduced herself.

"Hello. I'm Leslie O'Connor. May I help you?"

The man's eyes squinted, and he paused. "Actually, yes, I was looking for your office."

"Oh, how may I help you, Mr. . . . ?"

"I'm Nathan Welch. My daughter, Kaylee, is in Professor Langhorn's class. She said he treats her badly and singles her out in class every day. I want to know what you're going to do about this."

[Your response—What questions do you have of Mr. Welch? How does FERPA play into this scenario? In a follow-up, with what other persons would you communicate? What would you ask? What points would you wish to convey?]

Leslie then went to lunch with the Chamber of Commerce and made her twenty-minute presentation. She tried to mix in some humor and look professional at the same time. She talked about her background and the vision she was leading the university into this year.

But something special happened this day. Leslie sat at the head table with Dr. Dani Steele—the superintendent of the local school district. Dani was an impressive professional woman about ten years Leslie's senior. They quickly clicked, and Dr. Steele almost immediately became a mentor for Leslie.

(CS 13) CASE STUDY—ATHLETES SPECIAL TREATMENT—[NCAA]

Accounting Professor Meghan Ryan poked her head into Leslie's office.

"I'm sorry for interrupting, Dr. O'Connor, but I want to share a concern with you. I serve on the Admissions and Standards Committee of the faculty senate. I was told at yesterday's meeting that our admissions office staff discusses whether or not applicants are athletes when their committee deliberates over their decisions. I believe this is a violation."

Leslie sat stunned. "A violation of what?" she asked.

"I don't know if this is a violation of university policy or NCAA DIII rules. I was just told it was a violation," replied Professor Ryan.

"Hmm . . . I'll have to check into this."

> *[Your response—Is this, indeed, a violation of NCAA rules? What is your university policy on this matter? To whom would you speak? What questions do you have? If this is a violation, what would be your particular course of action? For further investigation—what is the authority or responsibility of the faculty in student admissions?]*

(CS 14) CASE STUDY—PERSONAL POLITICS IN CLASS— [POLICY—COMMUNICATION—FACULTY]

Leslie decided to take one last glance at her email before she left for the day. She had received a note written by a student. It read:

Dear Dr. O'Connor:
   I am a student in Professor Lehr's EDU 343 class. I and a number of my classmates are growing increasingly frustrated by his daily complaints against the Republican Party. He constantly derides anyone who is conservative or who would vote Republican. It's been getting worse these last two weeks. And I have evidence—I taped him saying these things. My parents and myself spend a great deal of money for me to attend this university. We don't pay for this kind of harassment. My fellow Young Republicans would like to speak with you at lunch on Monday, if you would agree.

Most sincerely,
Vince Bagley

[Your response—Write out your email response to Vince. Will you agree to meet with him and his peers? What is your institutional policy on professors speaking about politics in the classroom? How does academic freedom enter into this? Whom will you speak with about this concern?]

(CS 15) CASE STUDY—CONFEDERATE FLAG—[POLICY—ETHICS—COMMUNICATION]

Finally leaving the campus for the day, Leslie drove past several dorms. She noticed a Confederate flag hanging inside one of the dorm room windows. That angered her; surely this couldn't be allowed. She made a mental note to herself as to where the room was located and in which residence hall. She was going to talk with someone about this the next day.

[Your response—Does your institution have any policies about what is permitted to be hung from dorm room windows? Should this be considered "free speech" and therefore permissible? Would you talk with anybody about this, or just drop it? Could a policy be written to mitigate the hanging of such symbols from dorm room windows?]

Chapter Five

Never a Dull Moment

(CS 16) CASE STUDY—SIDEWALK CHALK— [POLICY—STUDENTS]

The next day at work, Leslie was spending a few moments scanning the websites of other campuses to see what they were using as dashboards. A knock came at the door. Mary walked in and said a student was outside, wanting to talk with Leslie about student government advertising.

"Hello, Dr. O'Connor. I'm Samantha Greer. I am running for SGA president, and I want to use sidewalk chalk to put out my name and message. Is this permissible?"

Leslie responded, "I'm not sure what our policy is on that. Let me look into it and get back to you."

> *[Your response—What is your institution's policy on such "chalking" on campus? What other information do you need from Samantha? With whom would you speak? On your campus, who advises the SGA? Write an email response to Samantha once you decide the best course of action.]*

(CS 17) CASE STUDY—ENROLLMENT DATA SHARING— [POLICY—COMMUNICATION]

After Leslie finished sending Samantha her email, she saw a message pop up from Teresa Longstreet, the director of admissions.

> Dear Dr. O'Connor, the Faculty Senate Admissions Committee has asked me for our enrollment numbers, particularly the high school academic profiles of the students—in aggregate—that have been admitted this year. My speculation

is that they believe we are letting in too many underqualified students. How would you like for me to respond?

[Your response—What is your response to Teresa? Write out your email response to her. What are your institution's admissions standards and cutoffs? Is it proper to share aggregated student data like this with the faculty senate? If so, are there other data that could be/should be shared with them?]

(CS 18) CASE STUDY—TUTORING HELP—[POLICY—STAFF]

Leslie's next email came from Dr. Beverely Hightower, the coordinator of tutoring services.

> Dr. O'Connor: I'm absolutely swamped with demands for our tutoring services. We have been extremely successful in getting the message out to students about our services. In fact, we've tripled our inquiries. But with these significant increases in numbers of students asking for help, coupled with our new accreditation assessment requirements, I am unable to keep up with the workload. I'm not referring to me helping with tutoring. I'm referring to the workload of managing the cases, the paperwork, the communications, assessment, etc. I'm drowning. I need another staff member; a graduate assistant would be an alternative solution, but not my preference. Please help me help our students. This is a retention necessity!
>
> Thank you, Dr. Hightower

[Your response—Write out your email response to Beverely. What points do you want to make certain you cover? What questions do you have of her? What possible solutions can you provide? At your institution, how would you go about requesting a new staff or a graduate assistant position in the middle of the academic year?]

(CS 19) CASE STUDY—OUTSIDE WORK—[POLICY—FACULTY]

Leslie decided to eat lunch at the student commons. Upon sitting down, she was approached by Professor Hank Fayol of the School of Education and Human Services.

"Hello, Dr. O'Connor. Might I trouble you for a moment?"

As Leslie smiled politely, Dr. Fayol continued, "Dean Riley suggested I talk with you. I am teaching a full load next semester, plus a one-credit overload. Augusta College has now asked if I could teach an online course for them next semester. Will you grant me the opportunity? It's a course I have taught before, face to face."

Leslie paused for a moment. "I'll have to take a look at our policy and get back to you."

[Your response—What is your institution's policy? With whom would you speak? What further questions do you have? Do you have a form that needs to be completed? Write out a response to Dr. Fayol.]

(IB 19) IN-BASKET—CARE PACKAGES— [POLICY—EXTERNAL]

When Leslie returned from lunch she had a voice-mail message from Dirk Gabelson, the manager of the campus bookstore. She returned the call.

She began, "Hello, Dirk, this is Leslie O'Connor. I see that you called me."

"Ah yes, Leslie. Thanks for calling back so quickly. Here's my problem. For the last several years, we have provided families care packages for their students during finals week. By 'provide,' I mean that families can purchase fun care packages for their kids. We're all set to do that again."

"What a wonderful idea, Dirk!" came Leslie's reply.

"But I just learned that the student government is selling their own version of this idea. That's going to take business away from our campus store," Dirk stated with an exasperated tone.

[Your response—Finish the phone conversation with Dirk Gabelson. What else would you discuss with him? With what other persons would you speak? Are there any contractual concerns that must be observed? Take some time to figure out possible solutions.]

(CS 20) CASE STUDY—KIT/IPEDS—[POLICY— PLANNING AND DATA MANAGEMENT]

Ben Troulovetz stepped into Leslie's office. In his hand, he held a rather large document.

"Good afternoon, Leslie," Ben began.

"How are you doing, Ben?" replied Leslie.

"I'm alright. Listen, I have the annual KIT report for you. I'd like for you to review it, and then meet with Theresa Halprin to see how she puts together the IPEDS report."

Leslie didn't know what the KIT report was, but she didn't want to look ignorant in front of her boss. So she replied, "I'll get right on it, Ben. Thank you."

[Your response—With permission, review your institution's most recent KIT report. Then, interview your head of institutional research. Prepare questions for them about where they pull their data for their IPEDS report, which are subsequently used for the KIT and FIT reports.]

(CS 21) CASE STUDY—IRB—[POLICY—FACULTY]

As Leslie escorted Ben out of her office, she noticed Institutional Review Board chair and faculty member Neal Sheppard waiting to see her.

"Neal, come on in," Leslie began.

"Thank you for allowing me to stop in unannounced, Leslie. I was hoping I could catch you. I've heard you're almost impossible to see." Neal laughed.

"That's about right, Neal. What can I do for you?"

"Well, the IRB is always so busy with reviewing requests, but I think we take far too much time reviewing run-of-the-mill proposals. I've heard that most other institutions have an expedited process whereby the chair has unilateral authority to grant approval of simple requests and then take only the more difficult ones to the full committee. Would you permit us to do that?"

Leslie paused for a moment. "Could you prepare a very brief proposal for me to look at?" Leslie thought this might buy herself some time to look into this matter more thoroughly.

"Of course," replied Neal. "By the way, if you haven't received IRB training yourself, might I suggest you run through the tutorial for basic training? I can send you the link along with my proposal."

Leslie agreed.

[Your response—Examine your institution's IRB processes, policies, and protocols. Would you approve such an expedited process? If so, what parameters would you want included? If you have not done the online tutorial for IRB, you can take the time to do so.]

(CS 22) CASE STUDY—INTELLECTUAL PROPERTY— [POLICY—ETHICS—FACULTY]

Leslie returned to her computer to check her email. She read a note from Chemistry Department Chair Hans Vertbienen. It read:

Dear Dr. O'Connor:

One of my colleagues has inquired about intellectual property rights of faculty. I am uncertain about university policy and legal ramifications, so I am asking you. Said professor has been developing an online teaching manual that follows along with the research he has been doing in his lab these past several years. He wants to be certain that other professors won't be able to use his manual when teaching their own courses. Please advise.

[Your response—There will certainly be other questions to which you would like additional information regarding this matter. What are those questions? What is your institution's policies governing intellectual property? What are possible answers to Dr. Vertbienen's inquiry? Who "owns" these courses, and how is that determined?]

(IB 20) IN-BASKET—FOREIGN STUDENT IN DORMS—[POLICY—STUDENTS]

This email was followed by an email from Ms. SuYe Kim, the coordinator for study-abroad programs:

Dear Dr. O'Connor,
One of our students from Chile has been living in the dorms this year. She is a freshman. She received a note from the residence hall director that she would not be permitted to live in the dorms in the spring semester because she will only be taking ten credits. Apparently the threshold to live in the dorms is full-time status.
What can we do for her? Her family doesn't have the money to have her move off campus. This seems very unfair to me, and the girl is terrified right now. Please help us out!!!

[Your response—Write out an email response to Coordinator Kim. The response should contain both your answer and your rationale.]

(IB 21) IN-BASKET—ALUMNI OPPORTUNITY—[COMMUNICATION—EXTERNAL]

There was a knock on Leslie's open door. It was Mary.
"Hello, Leslie. Your appointment with Mr. Jerome May is here."
Leslie looked confused. "What appointment? Who is Mr. May?"
Mary responded, "Oh, Mr. May is the alumni director. He called while you were out and asked to schedule a short appointment with you, so I put him down for this time. Your calendar was clear. I hope this was okay."
Leslie thought, *No, this is not okay. We'll talk about this later.* But for now, she only said, "Sure, show Mr. May in."
Leslie began, "I remember you, Jerome. You were at my interview!"
"That's right, Leslie. It's such a pleasure to have you on board. I know your time is limited, so I'd like to jump right in. As you may or may not know, your predecessor wanted our two offices to start an alumni ambassador program. We would identify at least two ambassadors for every county

across the state, and several in other states. These ambassadors would help us connect to the communities, set up school visits and alumni events, and meet with potential donors. We would pay some sort of a stipend to each on an annual basis. With that said, I have already begun making many connections and have dozens of folks ready to serve as ambassadors. Now we need to start putting this into action, so I came to you for help with the next steps."

Leslie was both nervous and excited. This sounded like a wonderful opportunity, but it also sounded like a huge and complex undertaking.

[Your response—What questions do you have at this moment for Mr. May? What follow-up actions would you need to take?]

(CS 23) CASE STUDY—ADJUNCT PAY—[POLICY—FACULTY]

Ben Troulovetz stopped by unexpectedly to see Leslie. "Hello, Leslie. I have a task I'd like for you and Benzar to investigate. I'm getting a growing number of adjunct faculty complaining about the lack of pay increases. They tell me that not only have they not seen a pay raise for six years, their pay is out of whack compared to adjuncts at other colleges in the region. I'd like you and Benzar to see what other campuses are paying their adjuncts and what kind of pay structures they have in place. I'm not sure we shouldn't create something new."

[Your response—This case will take some time. Investigate how your institution pays its adjuncts and how this compares to other similar institutions in your area.]

(IB 22/CS 24) IN-BASKET AND CASE STUDY—ACADEMIC INTEGRITY—[POLICY—STUDENTS]

Less than an hour later, Dean Lizbeth Albertine knocked on Leslie's door. She appeared to be filled with anxiety and angst.

"What is wrong, Lizbeth?" started Leslie.

With an edge of anger in her voice, Dean Albertine began: "I and my faculty believe that students in two of our classes cheated on their midterm exams. Collectively, their midterm grades were far better than their early exam scores. All but two students scored in the mid- to upper-nineties. Their earlier exam scores were in the sixties to eighties with only a few nineties. We used a test bank, and we think that the students breached it. This is a clear violation of the code of conduct in our program. Each student signs an agreement of understanding after I discuss this policy with them. I think we need to expel all of these students!"

[Your response—What immediate questions do you have of Dean Albertine? Does your institution have a similar code of conduct? If so, does it give directions for adjudication? Assuming the students deny such a breach of the test bank, what would you do?]

(CS 25) CASE STUDY—ACADEMIC PROGRAM REVIEW—[POLICY—ACADEMICS]

Leslie returned to her computer and found a note from Dr. Miles Crenshaw, director of assessment and accreditation liaison. The email read:

Dr. O'Connor:
   At the end of the week, I would like to send each academic dean a copy of the policy for academic program review and corresponding template. I would like to have feedback from you as to whether you like it the way it is, or should we discuss any changes?
   Regards,
   Dr. Crenshaw

[Your response—Review your institution's academic program review procedures. Compare it with similar institutions. Are there any modifications you would like to see made?]

(IB 23) IN-BASKET—OVERRULED—[COMMUNICATION]

As you will recall, earlier [see Email 3] Leslie dealt with a J-Term student trip request from Professor Sesler. This email request is repeated below.

Email 3

Hello, Leslie:
   I want to run this idea past you early. Dr. Sesler (the associate professor of art history) will be leading a J-Term trip to Eastern Europe. He would like to take his son Kyle along. Kyle will be a first-semester freshman starting this coming spring. Would you permit him to go on the trip? We have two prohibitions that need to be considered. First, we typically do not allow family members to travel on these trips. Second, we do not permit students who haven't taken classes yet to go on these trips. I would like to support this request, but I do understand it could be a slippery slope. Thank you for your consideration.

You were asked to respond to this request.

Ms. SuYe Kim, the coordinator for the study-abroad program, stopped Leslie in the hallway. "Hello, Dr. O'Connor. I was surprised that Dr. Troulovetz overturned your decision about Dr. Sesler's request. Did you know about that?"

Leslie was caught off guard by this, and she didn't recall the circumstances. "What are you talking about, SuYe?"

Ms. Kim reminded Leslie of Dr. Sesler's request to take his son along on the J-Term trip to Eastern Europe. She then reminded Leslie of her decision at the time.

"You mean Ben overturned my decision?" questioned Leslie.

"Right. You didn't know that?" replied SuYe.

Leslie did not respond. She didn't know what to think.

[Your task—Review how you originally responded to Email 3. Then, for this activity, consider the fact that Dr. Troulovetz overturned your decision without communicating with you. How will you respond, specifically, about this? What do you plan to say or do?]

(IB 24) IN-BASKET—GRADE APPEAL/BELL CURVE— [POLICY—FACULTY/STUDENTS]

As Leslie walked back into her office, she noticed a student waiting for her. "Dr. O'Connor, I'm Ava Flowers. May I speak with you?"

Leslie was, of course, not going to turn a student away. "Of course, Ava. Please come on in. What brings you to my office?"

Ava began, "I just received my midterm grade from Professor Williams. He gave me a D. My percentage score is a seventy-eight percent. That is supposed to be a C+. I asked Dr. Williams why I was getting a D. He told me that he grades on the curve—whatever that means. It certainly doesn't seem fair to me. I cannot get a D in this class."

[Your response—How would you respond to Ava? Specifically, what would you say to her? Then, what would be your follow-up? Would you speak with the dean, the professor? What would you say? Are there any policies to check on?]

(CS 26) CASE STUDY—FINANCIAL AID DISCLOSURE/BEAUTY SCHOOL DROPOUT—[POLICY—STUDENTS]

No sooner had Leslie finished speaking with Ava than her phone rang.

"Hello, Leslie, this is Teresa Longstreet."

"Good afternoon, Teresa. How are things in Admissions?" came Leslie's response.

"Okay. But I have a bit of a problem. We have a student whom we recently admitted. However, when the financial aid office checked her FAFSA, they discovered that she did not disclose one of the schools she previously attended."

Leslie asked, "Why is that a problem?"

"Our policy states that if an applicant does not disclose all previous schools attended, their acceptance will be rescinded."

"Oh, that makes sense," replied Leslie. "So what's the problem?"

"Well, the school the student did not disclose was the Northern University of Cosmetology. So it's not a traditional college, nor is it accredited. She probably didn't even think it was a 'real' college—like us. So, does the policy take effect in this case or not? Also, it is our practice that all letters of revocation must come from your office."

[Your response—How would you respond in this case? What questions do you have? What factors need to be considered? Could there be any unintended consequences with your decision? Would an appeals process be appropriate?]

Chapter Six

When It Rains, It Pours

(CS 27) CASE STUDY—PROFESSIONAL DEVELOPMENT—
[POLICY—FACULTY]

One of the things that had interested Leslie most about Gulf Vista University was its faculty-led Teaching Excellence Center. However, this morning while she was drinking her coffee at home and reviewing its website, something concerned her. She was looking at recent faculty development awards given out by the TEC faculty committee; they seemed to be sponsoring faculty to attend professional conferences focused on their research, and not on pedagogy.

Leslie went back and reviewed the proposal guidelines; they stipulated that such grants were for the express purpose of improving teaching and learning, and they included a feedback loop in which the professor would present a workshop to colleagues about what they learned at the conference. This didn't seem to be the case with the recent awards, however; the practice seemed to focus on professors' research support as opposed to the support of instruction and student learning for everyone. She was going to look into this.

For now, it was time to get to work. With that, she hopped into her car and began the twenty-minute drive to campus.

[Your response—Examine your institution's teaching excellence center. Who is responsible for it? What is its mission, procedures, and policies? What is the administration's role in it? If you were in Leslie's shoes, how would you intervene if you had a concern?]

(CS 28) CASE STUDY—ASSAULT—[POLICY—STUDENTS]

Leslie liked to get to work before anyone else. This was the one time of the day she seemed to be able to control her schedule and get things done. However, this morning as Leslie walked to her office, she saw a student sitting on the floor just outside her door. The young woman looked like she hadn't slept, her hair was in disarray, and she looked very pale.

Leslie bent down slightly and inquired, "Is everything okay?"

The girl quietly shook her head, signaling that everything was not okay.

"Let's go inside my office," Leslie whispered.

As they were seated, Leslie asked, "What's wrong?"

The young woman finally lifted her head a bit, but she did not look Leslie in the eye. "I've seen you talking with students on campus before. I think I can trust you. I need to talk in complete confidentiality."

"I promise," replied Leslie.

"Oh, thank you, Mrs. O'Connor. My name is Mandi. I was at a party on campus last night, and I know I shouldn't have been drinking, but I know I didn't drink too much. I wasn't drunk. But somehow I passed out. I think someone put something into my beer. I woke up without any clothes on in a guy's bed—I don't know whose room it was. But I know I was raped. Some images of what happened keep popping back into my head, but they're cloudy. I just remember saying, 'No, no, no.'"

"Keep going, Mandi," Leslie urged, making sure she took copious notes.

[Your response—Write down your thoughts about how Leslie is handling this case. Review your policy and procedures about on-campus assault—including your responsibilities. Write out a statement describing what Leslie should have done from the beginning and how she should proceed. Could Leslie truly promise complete confidentiality? Is she a mandatory reporter?]

(CS 29) CASE STUDY—HAZING—[POLICY—COMMUNICATION—STUDENTS]

As Leslie escorted Mandi out of her office, she couldn't help but think, *This morning can't get off to any worse of a start*. But things weren't going to get any better. Professor Franklin was now sitting outside her office waiting to see her.

"Good morning, Dr. O'Connor. I am wondering if I might have a word with you," he began.

"Of course, please come in, Dr. Franklin."

"One of my freshman students, a male, came up to me after class. He is a soccer player, and he told me of some inhumane things that have been done to him and a couple of the other athletes. It's akin to hazing, and I must let someone know. So, unfortunately, it is you. Do with the information as you see fit, but I think we both agree this must stop immediately and the guilty parties must be redressed."

"Dr. Franklin, what happened?" Leslie implored.

"I'd rather not describe the incidents, and I don't fully know the details anyway. But it is safe to say that the boys were humiliated, and forced to do things that are sickening. And I heard this has been going on for the last few years, ever since the new soccer coach was hired. I must now go teach my next class."

> *[Your response—What further questions would you have for Dr. Franklin? Spend some time reviewing your institution's policies and procedures regarding hazing. How should this situation be handled? Now that Dr. Franklin has reported these practices to you, have his own responsibilities ceased?]*

(CS 30) CASE STUDY—SOCIAL MEDIA— [COMMUNICATION—POLICY—STAFF]

Mary walked into Leslie's office. "Excuse me, Dr. O'Connor. I have two items for you. First, I just received an anonymous complaint. I pressed the person for his name, but he wouldn't tell me."

"What was his concern, Mary?"

"He said he was on Facebook and noted that our associate registrar, Blue Thorndike, had posted some hateful speech on his personal page. He wrote, and I quote, 'The POTUS continues his empty-headed rhetoric against people of color, and he must stop on all counts! Join me in this call!' The anonymous caller wants him fired—now."

Leslie didn't know how to respond. She finally said, "Okay, I'll look into it. Did they want any kind of callback or anything?"

"No, just for Blue to be fired."

> *[Your response—What would be your course of action after receiving this information? Do you have any policies to help give you direction? With whom would you speak? What would you say to them?]*

(CS 31) CASE STUDY—BUDGET REQUEST— [COMMUNICATION—POLICY]

Mary continued, "The second item is that Dean Hakeem stopped by to talk with you. Since you were busy, he told me the main points."

Leslie said, "Go on, Mary."

"The Mass Comm. students submitted one of their projects to the National Mass Comm. Association . . . I can't remember what it's called . . . but they won second place! Their professor would like to take three students, and he would chaperone, to the awards event. He says this would bring great publicity for the university and it would be a great once-in-a-lifetime experience for the kids."

Leslie's eyes lit up. "Well, that's great news! Let's make this happen."

Mary paused. "I wish it was that easy. Neither the department nor Dean Hakeem has budgeted for this expense, which would cost roughly fifteen hundred dollars. Dean Hakeem is asking if you can pay for it from your budget."

The excitement left Leslie's face. "Do you know if we have any money in our own budget, Mary?"

"No, we didn't budget for any such event, either."

[Your response—In your own institution's budget, where could you look for help? How would you go about making a decision like this?]

(CS 32) CASE STUDY—STUDENT COURSE EVALUATIONS— [POLICY—COMMUNICATION—FACULTY/STUDENTS]

Turning back to her computer, Leslie saw an email from Faculty Senate Chair Barbara Bouche. It read:

> Dr. O'Connor, as you are the administrative representative to the senate, I have been asked to talk with you about revisiting the purpose and process of collecting student evaluations of faculty teaching. Might we schedule an appointment for later this week?
> Regards,
> Barbara Bouche, Faculty Senate Chair

[Your response—Review your institution's policies and procedures for collecting student feedback on their professors. Write a short statement about their strengths, where they are problematic, and ways in which they could be improved.]

(CS 33) CASE STUDY—TRANSGENDER STUDENT— [POLICY/ETHICS—STUDENTS]

This email was followed by another one, this time coming from Dean of Students Dr. Helga Korschvitz. In the email, she explained a vexing issue that had been raised to her earlier in the morning.

One of the students residing in the male dorms has been struggling with gender identity. "Phoenix" has decided to come out and embrace her gender as female. Her family has given mixed feedback, but she is meeting with a counselor and doing alright. The dilemma is that, while she remains anatomically a male, she wishes to move into one of the female residence halls. The university has not had to deal with such an issue yet, and the dean wants to discuss this with Leslie.

> *[Your response—Does your institution have any policies or protocols to help guide in decisions like this? What are all of the consequences that need to be considered in such cases? Who needs to be involved in creating a transgender policy and guidelines, in general, and how would you suggest the dean work with Phoenix and with the university staff in this particular case? What are the myriad issues involving transgender students on a residential campus? How do state laws impact these decisions?]*

(CS 34) CASE STUDY—SUNSETTING PROGRAMS—
[POLICY—ACADEMICS]

Another email awaited Leslie. This one was from her boss. In the email, Ben wrote:

> Leslie, President Boggs has asked us to examine low-enrolled academic programs and make suggestions for sunsetting those that have historically low enrollments and do not have clear plans to grow. Please work with the academic deans to examine our existing policies in this matter and make suggestions for those programs you would like to sunset.

> *[Your response—Examine your institution's policy for any academic program viability and sunset clause. If none exists, what should be considered in creating such a policy? Who should be involved in creating such a policy and in enforcing it?]*

(CS 35) CASE STUDY—AVERAGE CLASS SIZE—
[POLICY—ACADEMICS]

Ben's email triggered another question for Leslie. Recently, she had been reviewing the university's website and noticed two data points: average class size and faculty/student ratio. She had a general idea what these terms meant, but she wasn't quite sure how they were defined and calculated in this instance. Did these include all classes? Graduate classes? Was any of this information disaggregated? How were labs, studio courses, and independent studies calculated?

Leslie wrote to Dr. Halprin to find out.

[Your response—Talk with your director of institutional research at your university. Find out how these statistics are defined and determined. Then examine how they compare with your peers' results.]

(CS 36) CASE STUDY—LEADERSHIP PHILOSOPHY— [COMMUNICATION]

When she returned to her email, Leslie saw a note from Dean of Students Helga Korschvetz. Dr. Korschvetz had invited Leslie to give welcoming remarks to the new class of student leaders on campus. These twenty-five students had agreed to participate in a yearlong series of seminars and workshops to hone their leadership knowledge and skills.

[Your response—Write a five-minute-long welcoming speech—one that also describes your leadership philosophy and will inspire these future leaders.]

(CS 37) CASE STUDY—SEARCH AND SCREEN— [POLICY—STAFF]

As Leslie was leaving her office to go home for the night, she was stopped by Ben. He reported to Leslie that Dean Taylor of the library had spoken to him of her impending retirement earlier in the afternoon. Ben wanted Leslie to chair the search committee for her replacement.

[Your response—If you were to convene a search committee for a new dean of the library, whom would you include? Review your institution's policies and procedures for running a search committee. Put together a draft position announcement and determine the costs with a suitable marketing journal.]

Chapter Seven

Mother Never Said It Was Going to Be Easy

(CS 38) CASE STUDY—DIVERSITY IN THE CLASSROOM—
[POLICY—COMMUNICATION—FACULTY/STAFF]

The next afternoon, Leslie stopped over to Ben's office to give him a draft list of committee members, the position announcement, and the necessary pricing for such.

"Very good, Leslie. Go ahead and convene the ad hoc committee. But before you do so, where do you plan to go to reach out to underrepresented populations? I would like to have a well-qualified pool of applicants," noted Ben.

Leslie replied, "I'll work with HR to expand our reach to minority populations."

"Thank you, Leslie," came Ben's response. "This brings me to my next item. I would like you to also lead a task force to develop a plan on increasing both our minority faculty ranks, as well as our minority student population. You can have two months to share with me a report about your committee's ideas."

> *[Your response—If you were Leslie, what questions would you ask of Ben before you left his office? This case study could provide the perfect opportunity for a group reading this book to work together investigating what other universities are doing to increase minority hires and student numbers. Further, there is a great repository of ideas found in the professional literature. Take the time to examine this literature for ideas.]*

(CS 39) CASE STUDY—STUDENT COURSE EVALUATIONS—
[POLICY—FACULTY/STUDENTS]

As Leslie was walking back to her office, she was stopped by Faculty Senate Chair Dr. Barbara Bouche.

"Good morning, Leslie."

"Well, good morning to you, Dr. Bouche. You look like you're on a mission."

Dr. Bouche laughed. "As a matter of fact, I am on a mission of sorts. You see, the faculty senate has been disgruntled for quite some time with the end-of-semester course evaluations completed by students. Their concerns are about the validity and reliability of those evaluations."

"I understand," Leslie replied. "All faculties have these concerns."

"Our concerns, in particular, are that tenure-track faculty members are too lenient with their students in order to get good responses. In other words, they protect themselves from poor evaluations by lowering their standards."

"Again, I understand your concern," answered Leslie. "What would you like of me?"

"I'm glad you asked, Leslie. We've created an ad hoc committee to study this issue. We'd like you to serve in an ex officio capacity. Would you be willing to join us in uncovering faculty concerns, examining what our peers are doing, and seeing if we could come up with a better model?"

"I'd be happy to join you, Barbara."

[Your response—This would be another excellent case study to consider as a class. Each classmate should bring their respective student opinion surveys and compare and contrast them with each other. What are the best features of each? Do you have evidence of reliability and validity? What does the literature say about this topic? What weight should be given to these feedback surveys for faculty tenure, promotion, and renewal? And how can students be assured that results of these surveys matter, that they are not a waste of time?]

(CS 40) CASE STUDY—LOW-ENROLLED PROGRAMS—
[POLICY—ACADEMICS]

Leslie received an email from a former colleague. It was a delight to read a friendly note from her friend. Like most such notes, though, there was something more to the agenda. Her friend asked Leslie whether she knew anything about the Delaware Cost Study used to determine instructional costs and productivity. Leslie had not heard of such a study, but the thought was intriguing. She immediately went online.

[Your response—Visit the website. This case study could provide another good opportunity for the class to review key aspects of the Delaware Study of

Instructional Costs and Productivity. Do any of your institutions have similar approaches?]

(IB 25) IN-BASKET—FACULTY DISHONESTY—FRAUDULENT SYLLABUS—[POLICY—ETHICS—FACULTY]

As Leslie was reading about the Delaware Study, she heard a knock on her office door. It was Dean Riley from the College of Education and Human Services.

"Well, hello, Quentin. What brings you to my office today?"

Dean Riley looked grim. "Dr. O'Connor, I have a problem. I just don't know the magnitude of it."

The smile left Leslie's face. "What is it, Quentin? Please have a seat." She motioned to the chair in front of her desk, and she walked over and sat in the chair next to him.

"Well, one of our graduate assistants came into my office first thing this morning. He had a syllabus from Dr. Renfro he had been asked to copy for the students. But the GA said it didn't look anything like other syllabi Dr. Renfro had used previously. So he went online—and he found the exact same syllabus created by another professor in California. The only changes were the name of the professor, the school, the course name and number, etc."

"How could the GA figure this out and find the original?"

Dr. Riley explained, "Well, under the Recommended Readings section, the originating professor had written, 'my book.'" Quentin added, "This professor has no ties to our university. I can't tell you how upset I am with Renfro! I think this demands his immediate dismissal!"

Leslie's mouth fell open.

[Your response—How should you respond to Dean Riley at this moment? Do you have any other questions? What would you do in this situation? Is this an offense worthy of immediate dismissal? Has the professor done anything wrong?]

(CS 41) CASE STUDY—ADVANCEMENT FUND-RAISER— [COMMUNICATION—EXTERNAL]

Leslie returned to her email. After skipping through several less-pressing requests, she saw a red-flagged note from Shirlee Reed, vice president of advancement, marketing, and communications. The subject line read: "Your Assistance Required."

The body of the email went on:

President Boggs has asked me to meet with all senior-level administrators in order to put together an advancement plan for the purpose of dramatically increasing academic scholarships for students and professional development opportunities for faculty. My first order of business will be to meet with each of you individually, and then we will put together an ad hoc task force to address this task. Please contact my office to schedule a 1:1 appointment.

[Your response—Prepare a list of questions that you would like to ask the vice president of advancement to learn more about these responsibilities. Then actually schedule and conduct such an interview. See what ways you might get involved in fund development.]

Chapter Eight

Can I Get a Do-Over?

(IB 26) IN-BASKET—DEAN ARGUMENT—
TEMPERS—[COMMUNICATION—STAFF]

The next morning started off with Leslie leading her administrative council meeting. All went smoothly, until the topic of the new early alert program was broached by Dean of Students Helga Korschvitz.

Dr. Korschvitz began: "I am so pleased with our first foray into our electronic early alert system. The professors who are using it have really embraced this method of communicating their concerns to individual student advisors. I really think we can make a significant impact with these students—catch them before their problems become insurmountable. This could have a tremendous impact on student retention."

Several other deans nodded their heads. But Dean Albertine kept her head down. She never looked up, but her words were clear when she spoke. "My faculty will never participate in this early alert system!" she snapped quite angrily.

The meeting came to a halt. Everyone froze.

Dr. Korschvitz gathered herself somewhat and responded, "I'm sorry. I didn't know there was a problem, Lizbeth."

"It's a huge waste of my faculty's time. They were never asked for their input before this system was purchased, and it has too many bugs in it!" Dr. Albertine's tone had not changed.

All eyes of the administrative council members turned to Leslie.

[Your response—You don't have time to think. You need to respond somehow on the spot, just like Leslie did. With this in-basket response, you have two options: either write down how you would handle this and what you would say,

or role-play the scenario with a group of peers. At a later time, determine how you would seek to resolve this issue.]

(CS 42) CASE STUDY—FACEBOOK REQUEST—[COMMUNICATION—ETHICS—STUDENTS]

Leslie noticed she had a Facebook friend request. It was from Gabriel Alvarez—one of the students who had participated in her interview. She often saw and interacted with Gabriel on campus. Leslie wondered, *Should I accept a student's friend request?*

> [Your response—Should Leslie accept this friend request? What kinds of issues should she consider before making this decision? Should she accept friend requests from coworkers or subordinates? Facebook is only one social media platform. What about LinkedIn and others?]

(CS 43) CASE STUDY—ANONYMOUS COMPLAINT—[ETHICS—COMMUNICATION—STAFF]

As Leslie returned to her office after lunch, she noticed a plain white envelope resting on her chair. On it read the words, "Dr. O'Connor—Confidential," handwritten in pencil. She opened the envelope to see these penciled words: "Ben T. is having an affair with one of our staff members. This is killing morale. Please help."

> [Your response—How would you handle this situation?]

(CS 44) CASE STUDY—SPECIAL TREATMENT FOR ATHLETES—[NCAA]

Leslie sat stunned at her desk; no one else had yet returned from lunch. While her mind was racing with thoughts about what to do, there came a knock at her door. It was a student whom Leslie did not recognize.

"May I help you?" asked Leslie.

"Hello, ma'am. My name is Latfa, and I'm a student in Professor Simmons's Biology 220 class. It seems unfair to me and some of my classmates that Professor Simmons allows the athletes to choose their assignments, while the rest of us have no choice."

"What do you mean, Latfa, that the athletes get to choose their assignments?" asked Leslie.

"The athletes can either do the assignment the rest of us do, or they can read an article on the topic and write a critique, for example. I think we should all get to choose, or the athletes should be required to do what the rest of us must do. In fact, is this not a violation of NCAA rules?" queried Latfa.

[Your response—What other questions would you have for Latfa? How would you finish the conversation? Is this, indeed, a violation of NCAA rules? What further questions do you have, and to whom would you address them?]

(CS 45) CASE STUDY—KENTE STOLE—[COMMUNICATION—POLICY—STUDENTS]

The next appointment on Leslie's calendar arrived on time. It was SGA President Xena Washington.

"Come on in, Xena. It is wonderful to see you this morning. How are you doing?" queried Leslie.

"I'm doing quite well, Dr. O'Connor," came Xena's reply. "In fact, that is why I'm here. I will actually be graduating early."

"That's fantastic, Xena. I'm so happy for you, but I certainly will miss your leadership on this campus."

Xena continued, "Thank you, Dr. O'Connor. I have friends at other colleges who they tell me they are permitted to wear Kente stoles at graduation. I'm asking permission for our African American students to also wear Kente stoles."

"What is a Kente stole?" asked Leslie.

"They are typically brightly colored stoles worn at graduation to honor our African heritage. Different colors and designs have different significance. These are very special to our families and are worn with pride. Registrar Suarez said we aren't allowed to wear anything beyond university-approved regalia. So I am requesting your permission for me and for my fellow African American students to wear these Kente stoles that represent our heritage."

Leslie paused, not knowing what to say. Finally she replied, "I don't have an answer for you at this moment, Xena. Please allow me to look into your request and get back to you. I promise to have a response of some sort for you by the end of the week."

[Your response—Do you have any particular feelings about this issue? Would you prefer to allow this request, or not? What questions would you seek to have answered, and whom would you ask? Are you afraid of risking a slippery slope by allowing this request, causing other requests to be made? How should such decisions be made?]

(IB 27) IN-BASKET—SOCIAL MEDIA IN THE WORKPLACE—[COMMUNICATION—ETHICS/POLICY—STUDENTS/STAFF]

As Leslie escorted Xena from her office, she continued across the hall to the washroom. She then decided to do a "walk-by" several offices. As she walked by the financial aid office, she noticed that the student worker there was sending a message through Facebook on her office computer. Leslie kept walking, but it bothered her more and more. She finally turned around and walked back into the financial aid office.

Leslie walked over to the student and stated, "It's not appropriate for you to be using a work computer during work hours to engage with social media."

To Leslie's surprise, the student seemed a bit taken aback. "What do you mean? Everyone does it!"

Now Leslie was on her heels. "I can assure you, not everyone does it. I'm telling you that this is unacceptable behavior from our student workers."

The student didn't back down. "I'm not just talking about student workers. I'm talking about your employees. I bet you could go into any office on this campus and find that half of the employees are on social media at any given time."

Leslie could feel her face turning red. She didn't need a student to speak to her in this manner, nor was this social media engagement behavior tolerable. "I'm telling you right now, you are not permitted to be on social media while using a work computer, during work hours, and getting paid."

The student had a stone-cold look on her face, but she closed out of her Facebook account. Leslie turned on her heel and marched out of the office.

> *[Your response—Did Leslie handle this situation appropriately? Is there anything you would add to the conversation? What would be your next step? Would you conduct a policy review? Would you talk with anyone in particular?]*

(CS 46) CASE STUDY—STARTING A NEW STUDENT ORGANIZATION—[POLICY—STUDENTS]

Leslie scurried back to her office; she knew that Kyle Franklin—the captain of the football team—had scheduled an appointment to meet with her.

Indeed, when she entered her office, Kyle was there. The football player got up from the chair, walked across the room, and firmly shook Leslie's hand. As they did so, Kyle looked squarely into Leslie's eyes and said, "Thank you for meeting with me, Dr. O'Connor. As I promised you several weeks ago, I am back to talk with you about starting an affiliated group with the Fellowship of Christian Athletes."

Leslie had not known the topic of today's meeting beforehand, so she sat down with Kyle to learn of his intentions, the level of student interest, who he thought might serve as the faculty or staff advisor, potential charter requirements, any budget requirements, etc.

Kyle didn't have all the answers to her questions, and Leslie didn't know the protocol for starting a new student organization. They both agreed to meet the following week, after they each had a chance to do some research on the issues.

[Your response—Review your institution's policy for starting a new student organization. With whom would you speak? Is there a form that needs to be completed, any meetings/fora that must occur?]

(CS 47) CASE STUDY—ONLINE INSTRUCTION— [POLICY—ACADEMICS—COMMUNICATION]

Ever since Leslie had arrived on campus, she had been concerned about the quality of the online instruction. This concern was not unique to Gulf Vista—it was a concern that she had had for years. So she stepped into the outer office to question Mary.

"Mary, who is our director of instructional technology?"

Mary looked quizzically at Leslie. "I'm not sure what you mean, Dr. O'Connor. Irving McMaster is our vice president for information technology."

"No," Leslie continued. "Who is responsible for *instructional* technology? You know, the learning management system, online and hybrid instruction, oversight, and so on?"

"Oh, I see, I think," Mary replied. "We don't have any one person responsible for that. I guess those issues are left up to the college deans, working in concert with Mr. McMaster."

Leslie stood stunned for a moment. "Hmm . . . I'm going to have to do some digging into this." With that said, she walked back into her office and looked out the window. She decided she was going to have to talk with someone, but whom? And what was she going to ask?

[Your response—With whom would you start such a conversation? What would you want to know about quality assurance and accountability? About what other things would you like to know more? Note: GVU does, in fact, have a person responsible for instructional technology—it's noted elsewhere in this book.]

(CS 48) CASE STUDY—O CHRISTMAS TREE—
[POLICY—COMMUNICATION—STAFF]

There came a knock on Leslie's door. Apparently, Mary had stepped out of the office, so no one was there to screen walk-ins.

Leslie queried, "Hello?"

A man poked his head around the door. Leslie recognized the face, but didn't know who it was.

"Hello, Dr. O'Connor. Might I have a few minutes of your time?" came the reply.

Leslie wanted to say no. But she knew that was not the correct response. "Please come in." She stood and motioned the gentleman to one of the chairs on the other side of her desk. They shook hands. "I'm Isaac Jacobson. I work in Accounts Payable down the hall."

"Oh, yes! Isaac, it's good to meet you! What brings you over to my office?"

"Well, it's a concern that I have had for years, but no one has taken the time to really listen to me before. Oh, by the way, I must say I have watched you from afar. You treat people so wonderfully, and you have earned your reputation as a good-hearted soul."

Leslie gave a pleasant smile. "You are too kind, Mr. Jacobson. But what is troubling you?"

"Yes, yes. Dr. O'Connor, if I may. . . . You see, I'm of the Jewish faith. I respect people of all faiths, and mine is so important to me, as I am sure yours is to you. Yes?"

Leslie did not respond other than giving him a polite smile. "Go on, Isaac."

"Well, you see, this university—in practice—is not secular. It clearly is a Christian university, almost to the exclusion of all other faiths."

Leslie didn't know what to say. She squinted and noted, "I don't follow you. People of all different faiths are welcome here. We don't discriminate based upon religion, and we host a number of cross-cultural events. I just don't follow."

Mr. Jacobson pursed his lips, but he met Leslie with kind eyes. He had obviously had this conversation before. "Please allow me to explain by way of some examples. If you go into most of the offices here in December, you will see Christmas decorations and Christmas trees, and you can hear Christmas carols being played in the background. I have even seen people with crosses on their desks and plaques with verses of scripture from the Bible."

Leslie rested her chin on her fingertips and looked up at Isaac as if she was asking what he actually wanted of her.

He continued, "Dr. O'Connor, I think our university family should acknowledge the fact that tacitly, subliminally, we are a Christian organization.

These seemingly innocuous things all together add up to a culture supporting one faith exclusively, and therefore it is not inclusive of other faiths."

Now Leslie certainly didn't know how to respond. She took a pregnant pause, not because she wanted to make a point, but quite simply because she didn't know what to say. Then—"What exactly are you asking of me, Mr. Jacobson?"

Isaac smiled. "In all honesty, I don't know. I've never gotten this far in this conversation with anyone before. Maybe a group of us could talk with some of the administrators. There are so many people—both staff and students—of different faiths. I know many of us feel the same way."

"Fair enough," Leslie replied. "Let me speak with the provost."

With that, Isaac got up and shook Leslie's hand. "I thank you for your time, Dr. O'Connor." He then let himself out.

[Your response—Does Isaac's argument have any merit? Do you feel your institution might make other non-Christian faiths feel unwelcome by inadvertently supporting Christianity? How would you continue this discussion on your campus?]

(CS 49) CASE STUDY—STAFF COUNCIL— [POLICY—COMMUNICATION—STAFF]

Isaac hadn't even made it out of the office suite before he popped his head back in. Leslie had a vision of Lieutenant Columbo of the famous seventies hit television show.

"Dr. O'Connor, while I still have you: a perfect vehicle or venue for such a discussion might be the staff council."

"What a great idea, Isaac!" came Leslie's reply. "Could you take this topic to the staff council for us?"

"Well, you see, that's the problem. We don't have a staff council. But we should!"

Leslie sat back down in her chair, exasperated.

[Your response—Does your institution have a staff council? If so, review their bylaws. What is their charge? Who makes up their membership? What authority do they have? Take the time to be a guest at one or two of their meetings. Better yet, serve as an administrative representative on the staff council.]

(PR 1) PHILOSOPHICAL REFLECTION— POWER AND AUTHORITY

Leslie was exhausted from the hectic pace of the day, but she had been looking forward to her dinner engagement that evening with Dani Steele. It seemed funny to her—two high-powered women lounging at Leslie's home in blue jeans and sweaters, eating take-out pizza.

After the better part of an hour of idle chitchat about their workday lives and summer vacation plans, Dani asked Leslie whether she felt she was able to accomplish all the things she had hoped to complete at this point in her new job.

At first, Leslie began talking about her accomplishments, but she then fell silent for a few moments. "I don't know, really, Dani. I mean, I am working so hard, getting so much work done, but I don't feel like I really have any power—I don't know if I really am a leader."

"I think I understand you, Leslie. But I bet if you asked your colleagues, especially those people who report to you, they would definitely say you're a leader," came Dani's response.

"That might be true. I just don't know. I mean, you're a superintendent. When you tell people to do something, they listen and they do it!"

Dani almost choked on her pizza. "You've got to be kidding me, Leslie! Do you really think that's the case? In fact, I often feel totally powerless myself. How can I tell if I really impact any students' lives? How can I tell whether I'm making a difference?"

Leslie looked stunned. "I can't believe I'm hearing you say that, Dani. Of course you make a huge difference in so many people's lives."

"How do you know? You can't prove it."

Again, Leslie looked stunned, and she sat there with her eyes squinted in disbelief. Here, Dani was the most impressive woman she knew, and yet her new friend was telling her that she was questioning her own leadership.

Dani continued, "When I taught in the classroom, it was very clear to me that I was making a difference in those kids' lives. I felt good about the impact I was making, and I knew I had made the right career choice. So I became a principal. Things changed. I worked less and less directly with the students, and I couldn't really tell if I was making a difference in those kids' lives anymore."

"Maybe that's kind of what I'm feeling," Leslie posited. "Still, when you were a principal, you could tell teachers what to do and they did it. I can't tell our faculty what to do and expect they will do it. They would laugh me off campus. You see, things are different in college. Faculty own the curriculum—they are the experts. It's not as simple as it is in K–12."

"Hold on for a minute, Leslie. I think you might have some misperceptions about K–12. Teachers still feel quite independent and make many choices of their own when it comes to their classrooms. Unions make the situation even more difficult."

"Go on," was all Leslie could muster.

"Listen, let me give you a concrete example. When I was a principal, I could tell teachers to hand in their lesson plans every Friday before they would leave for the weekend. I could also tell them what kinds of structure I wanted to see in their lesson plans—and they would do it."

"That's what I mean, Dani! It is different in K–12."

"Please let me finish, Leslie. I had the *authority* to require those things, and they would do it. But come Monday morning, they would close their classroom doors and teach whatever they wanted to teach and however they wanted to teach it. So I had legitimate authority, but did I really have any *power*? Power is about getting people to do what you want them to really do."

"Well, okay," Leslie followed, "but how did you get that power?"

"It wasn't easy. That power came by me talking with those teachers every day, by building relationships. It took time. Heck, it took years. It took hours and hours over months to talk about what was important to us in terms of our teaching, and in terms of student learning. We had to talk about what we valued and what we believed. It took faculty meetings filled with such dialogue, and it took countless one-on-one chats with teachers."

Leslie began to smile, but it was a smile filled with uncertainty. This sounded truly powerful, but more work than she thought.

"So, if after months and months of such deep and important discussions, I would ask faculty to hand in their lessons plans, I could feel confident about what they wrote and what they would do on Monday mornings. That, Leslie, is power. I could make a difference as a building leader. I could sway their thinking by having those hard and energetic discussions. And they, in turn, could sway me!"

"Dani, what a fantastic example! In fact, if you ask me, you actually gained more power by giving it away. In other words, by empowering your teachers, you got more power. Wow! This is awesome. Seriously, you make me think that I can really make a difference!"

[Your response—Do an exercise of free-flow or stream-of-consciousness thinking. Write down your thoughts as to how you could begin deliberately empowering others in order to really make a difference in the lives of your staff, faculty, and students.]

Chapter Nine

With a Renewed Sense of Optimism

(CS 50) CASE STUDY—SPLIT VOTE ON
TENURE—[POLICY—FACULTY]

As Leslie walked from the parking lot to the administrative building the next morning, she was joined by Dean Albertine.

"Good morning, Leslie," Lizbeth began.

"Good morning, Lizbeth. It looks like you have something on your mind."

"Well, Leslie, as a matter of fact, I do. Let me bend your ear for a moment."

Leslie laughed. She knew with Lizbeth it would be more than a moment. "Go on."

"As you are aware, each college's tenure committees are meeting presently and deliberating about tenure and promotion decisions. We have a problem with a nursing program decision. Dr. Renoir has a split vote of four-four. I'm planning on making the final decision, but this is a perennial problem with the nursing faculty. Half of our faculty are hard-core researchers. They strenuously believe that all faculty members must publish or perish when it comes to tenure decisions. The other half of the faculty argue just as strenuously that nursing is a different beast. Traditional research is not what is important. Rather, clinical practice is what is crucial. We go 'round and 'round each year with these arguments. And the junior faculty members get caught in the middle. I'm not asking you to do anything, but I just wanted to give you a heads-up."

Leslie smiled. "Actually, I have experience with this issue, Lizbeth. The nursing dean at my former institution encountered this same battle. I don't have a short-term solution for this particular instance, but I think I can help with a long-term solution." She winked.

"Oh, please do tell!"

"It begins at the beginning—even before the point of hire. When a position opens up, you and your faculty must agree ahead of time what the tenure expectations should be. Will there be primarily traditional scholarship-based expectations for tenure, or primarily clinical-based expectations? This, then, gets put in each new hire's job description and subsequently into the job postings."

"Leslie, we do that right now. We put both down as expectations."

Leslie quickly interjected, "But you can't have it both ways. You will need to choose. Let me go on, though. At the point of hire, I recommend that you, your chair, and the newly hired junior faculty member prepare a letter of expectations. In the letter, you will lay out precisely what is expected in terms of teaching, scholarship or professional expectations, and service. These could be further delineated annually as steps along the way toward renewal, promotion, and tenure. Then, each of you can sign it. I've seen it work, Lizbeth!" Leslie smiled, proud of herself.

"You know, that just might work, Leslie. I'm going to bring that up at my next faculty meeting. But that doesn't resolve my present dilemma."

At that, Leslie arrived at her office door. Her day had not officially begun yet, but it really had. "Sorry about that, Lizbeth. You're on your own with that problem."

> [Your response—What do you think of Leslie's solution? Do you have any other solutions? This would be a perfect topic to use to see what other peers' experiences have been at their institutions.]

(CS 51) CASE STUDY—TUTORING LOWERS GRADES?—
[POLICY/ETHICS—COMMUNICATION—FACULTY]

Leslie sat down at her desk and logged on to her computer. After deleting the numerous vendor requests, she opened her first official email of the day. It was from Beverely Hightower. It read:

Subject: Tutoring Demerits?
Dr. O'Connor:
    This matter was brought up to me yesterday morning. I have been so furious about it, I decided to wait until this morning to write to you!
    It was brought to my attention by a student that his course grade in Dr. Vertbienen's class was reduced by a full letter grade because the student received tutoring help. This made no sense to me, so I called Dr. Vertbienen. Indeed, the student was correct! Dr. Vertbienen had the temerity to tell me that he would not give any student who received assistance the grade they would

have gotten otherwise. In other words, if a student earned an A in his course, they would automatically be given a B simply because they were "given help." He further told me that he has always done this. This is totally unacceptable, and it must be addressed. These grades must be corrected. I don't even know what should be done about past grades!

Regards, Dr. Hightower

Leslie about passed out. What was she going to do?

[Your response—What would you do? Is this practice ethical? Would you call Dr. Hightower to get more information? If so, what would you ask? Would you next go to Dr. Vertbienen or his dean? What would you say and ask? Do you have the authority to change grades? How would you handle the issue of past grades? What are all of the issues that must be considered?]

(IB 28/CS 52) IN-BASKET AND CASE STUDY— CHANGING TRADITION/SYMBOLS—[COMMUNICATION]

Leslie was surprised when President Boggs entered her office.

"Good morning, Leslie. How are you doing this fine morning?"

"Well, good morning, President Boggs. I'm doing quite well. And how about you?"

"Say, Leslie, I've got a major favor to ask of you. I need someone who does not bring any historical bias or preconceived preferences about symbolism at Gulf Vista. You're relatively new here, and so you don't have the historical baggage that others might have."

Leslie didn't know what to say. She just sat there looking at Dr. Boggs.

Finally, President Boggs continued, "For several years, there have been rumblings from staff, students, and even alumni about our school mascot. They just don't like it. They want something more exciting and contemporary. On the other hand, there are also many steadfast loyalists who love our mascot and hold to the notion that that is who we are. But now even our school colors are being questioned. I'd like for you to put together a team of folks to make a recommendation to me about whether to keep or change our mascot and school colors. Let's try to get this accomplished by the end of next month."

[Your response—What questions do you have for Dr. Boggs? With whom would you immediately begin to speak? What are all the ramifications you would need to consider? Take fifteen minutes to jot down the questions you would have for Dr. Boggs before he leaves your office. Then, within that same fifteen minutes, begin to jot down a list of tasks and individuals with whom you would need to communicate. When it comes to changing a symbol of an institution, part of its heritage, what all needs to be considered? Whose views need to be considered?]

(IB 29) IN-BASKET—DEFAULT RATE—
[POLICY—ACADEMICS—COMMUNICATION]

Mary poked her head into Leslie's office. "Excuse me, Dr. O'Connor, but Kimberly Grasse is here to see you from Financial Aid."

Kimberly walked in slowly. "Good morning, Kimberly. What brings you here?" Leslie began.

"Well, our auditors are finishing up their annual on-site review, and they seem to have a 'finding,'" Kimberly stated.

"What 'finding'?" Leslie followed.

"Apparently our student loan default rate is of concern to them. It is much larger than it has been in the past."

> *[Your response—How would you continue this conversation with the director of financial aid? What else do you need to ask her before she leaves? In other words, what else do you need to learn about the situation right away?]*

(CS 53) CASE STUDY—LETTER OF REPRIMAND—
[POLICY/ETHICS—COMMUNICATION—STAFF]

After Leslie and Kimberly concluded their discussion, Leslie turned her attention back to her computer. Leslie had set it to "*ping*" every time Ben sent an email to her. This time his email subject line read: "Letter of Reprimand."

Leslie scrolled through the email, which included an attachment of a screenshot.

> Dr. O'Connor:
>
> It has been brought to my attention that Associate Registrar Blue Thorndike has posted an inappropriate commentary on his Facebook page. While employees certainly have the right to post whatever they wish on their personal websites, Mr. Thorndike lists on his Facebook page that Gulf Vista University is his employer and that he serves as associate registrar here.
>
> With that said, please write a letter of reprimand to place in his file, stating that such conduct is inappropriate and that any such future behavior may lead to the termination of his contract. Further, he should remove GVU as his employer on his social media pages if he plans to continue such political rants.
>
> Please see the screenshot I have attached: "POTUS is a race-baiter, and idiot, and evil. Fight fire with FIRE!"

> *[Your response—What other information about this situation do you need to know? Write a sample letter of reprimand. List the issues you would address with Blue when you formally meet with him to give him the letter of reprimand.]*

(CS 54) CASE STUDY—NATIONAL CLEARINGHOUSE—
[POLICY—ACADEMICS—COMMUNICATION]

This email from Ben was directly followed by another one from him. The subject line on this was "National Clearinghouse."

> Leslie, I just received an email from the president's LISTSERVE to which I belong. Basically, the question posed to the LISTSERVE is, "How does your institution use the National Clearinghouse? What information do you send to them? Who sends the information? And, most importantly, what information do you use from the Clearinghouse?" Please check with our admissions office for these answers and get back to me by the end of the week.
>
> *[Your response—What is the National Clearinghouse? Seek out the answers posed by Ben above, and prepare a memo in response.]*

(CS 55) CASE STUDY—PELL GRANTS—
[POLICY—ACADEMICS—COMMUNICATION]

The email from Ben about the Clearinghouse was followed by yet another email from him. This time the subject line read "Pell Grants."

> Hello, Leslie. Another LISTSERVE question focused on Pell Grants. Specifically, what has our Pell Grant rate been over the past five years? What is the trend? Do we offer special incentives and/or programs for these students? Also, what are the retention and graduation rates for these students? Again, a response by the end of the week is needed.
>
> *[Your response—Answer Ben's questions from this email as they relate to your present institution. Then prepare a memo in response.]*

(CS 56) CASE STUDY—INSTRUCTIONAL TECHNOLOGY PLATFORM—[ACADEMICS]

A new email popped up on Leslie's screen, but this one came from Ken Verkesne. The subject line read "Instructional Technology Platform."

> Good morning, Dr. O'Connor:
>   Our present LMS is old and getting out-of-date. In fact, we are several upgrades behind. Before we invest in the most recent upgrade, however, I think it would be beneficial to investigate other LMS to see what might be best for GVU. With your permission, I would like to convene an ad hoc committee and move forward with this process.
> Sincerely,
> Ken Verkesne

Director of Instructional Technology

[Your response—Write an email response to Ken. What do you need to ask him in this email, and what points should you make certain are addressed?]

(CS 57) CASE STUDY—NONTRADITIONAL STUDENTS— [PLANNING—STUDENTS]

Unbelievably, yet another email from Ben popped up on Leslie's screen. She was not liking this trend. The subject line of this email read, "Nontraditional Students."

> I promise, Leslie, that this will be my last email of the day. This query, too, is from my presidents' LISTSERVE. The focus is on nontraditional students. Specifically, they are asking what percentage of our student population are nontraditional students, what special recruiting efforts we have in place for these students, what special support systems we have in place for nontraditional students, and what our retention and graduation rates are for nontrads? As with the other emails, please see if you can respond by the end of the week.
> Best regards, Ben

[Your response—Instigate these questions posed by Ben as they relate to your own institution. How does your school define "nontraditional students"? Write an email response to Ben.]

(PR 2) PHILOSOPHICAL REFLECTION— MOTIVATION PRINCIPLES

Leslie felt a sense of relief when it was finally time to meet Dani Steele at the campus coffee shop. They had planned for this brief respite during their time together over the weekend. They hadn't planned on talking about anything in particular; it was just a chance to get away and chat.

They began by talking about a myriad of topics—vacation plans, issues at work, the weather, plans for the upcoming weekend. Then Leslie noticed a sense of angst from Dani.

"Leslie, I can't tell you how frustrated I am with our faculty and our school board members. We've had acrimonious relationships for years, and there has been downright hostility when it comes to contract negotiations. They treat each other as adversaries."

"Isn't that just the normal state of affairs between teacher groups and their bosses?" came Leslie's quick response.

"I sure hope not," continued Dani. "At least that's not what I expect under my leadership. I want us all to work together on the same team—even with tough issues. I just can't seem to motivate them to want to come together."

"That's really interesting that you say that, Dani. You make it sound as if you are responsible for professionals' motivation. Is that really your responsibility?"

There was an extended pause as Dani took a long sip of her peppermint mocha. She squinted her eyes at Leslie. "I don't know . . . I don't know."

Leslie replied, "At my former institution, a colleague mentioned to me that we are not responsible for other people's motivation. They are. As leaders, we are only responsible to help set the conditions for them to be self-motivated, to be intrinsically motivated. You get more when people are intrinsically motivated."

Dani came back immediately, "Well, how do you know what motivates people intrinsically?"

"Easy. You ask them. In fact, that's really the only way. Each person is unique, and so is their sense of motivation. We can't take a one-size-fits-all approach."

"So, how does that look with respect to my situation? I have two traditionally adversarial groups that I need to pull together. How can I motivate them to come together?"

"Again, you can't, Dani. You can only help them motivate themselves. Start asking them what they are trying to accomplish. Ask them both individually and collectively."

"You just said it was easy, Leslie."

"The idea is easy, Dani. The process is not," came Leslie's less-than-hopeful response.

> *[Your response—Begin by reexamining the response you wrote out in the introduction to this book. How has it changed? As a leader, is it your role to motivate people extrinsically? If so, how would you do this? If it's your role to set the conditions whereby professionals can be intrinsically motivated, how would you do that? Take some time to think of a situation in which you would have to pull people together and the role you would need to take in their motivation. Or you could try to respond to the situation in which Dani has found herself.]*

(CS 58) CASE STUDY—SUMMER BRIDGE— [ACADEMICS—STUDENTS]

When Leslie returned to her office, she turned her attention to her computer. Several emails had come through over the last ninety minutes.

Dr. Eugene Golden, the director of enrollment management, sent Leslie an email. It read:

> Dr. O'Connor, when you interviewed with us, you mentioned your thoughts on a summer bridge program for incoming students who are deemed as needing a

little extra boost in preparation for college. Our enrollment management team thinks your ideas have great merit, and we would like to discuss your thoughts and our thoughts, together. Might we be able to get together soon to chat?

[Your response—What are your thoughts about a summer bridge program? What concerns do you have? What things need to be considered, and if a new program was to be implemented, what issues should be addressed?]

(CS 59) CASE STUDY—ADMINISTRATOR PERFORMANCE REVIEWS—[POLICY—STAFF]

Mary knocked on the door. Leslie welcomed the interruption from her emails. Her lengthy to-do list was becoming a strain.

Mary began, "Dr. O'Connor, I have a tickler file to remind you that it's time for you to begin the annual performance reviews for all the deans and directors who report directly to you. Please let me know if I can be of any assistance in this."

Leslie held up her finger. "Actually, yes, Mary. Please give me a copy of each individual's performance review from last year. That's where I would like to begin." Leslie knew she did not need to reinvent the wheel, and this strategy would also give her the opportunity to see what process existed at GVU for such performance reviews.

[Your response—Take a look at your present institution's model for administrator performance review. Is it more narrative- or form-based? What types of evidence is necessary? Does it focus on goals and performance? Does one year lead into the next year? Is there any merit pay related to performance? How would you change your present system?]

(CS 60) CASE STUDY—RESPONSIBILITY-CENTERED MANAGEMENT—[POLICY—PLANNING]

Strange, but sometimes unrelated topics just popped into Leslie's head. She thought this might be a sign of creativity, but it was also annoying at times. In this particular instance, she remembered an earlier conversation with Library Dean Taylor. In fact, it had been during her interview. Dean Taylor had asked Leslie about her knowledge and experience with RCM—Responsibility-Centered Management. Leslie had not heard of it before, but she remembered it was related to some sort of budget model.

[Your response—Investigate the RCM budget model. You can learn more about it by visiting the website provided in the references listed in the back of the book. Jot down some notes, and talk with your mentor about the model and how it compares to the model you use.]

(CS 61) CASE STUDY—STUDY AWAY— [ACADEMICS—STUDENTS]

That was about all Leslie could handle for the time being. She decided to take a walk to a nearby deli, across from the campus, for lunch. As she walked in, SuYe Kim spotted her and motioned for Leslie to join her and her assistant for lunch. Leslie sat down after exchanging a few pleasantries.

"It's fortuitous that you would stumble upon us today, Dr. O'Connor. Nikki and I were just brainstorming ideas about how to improve the stagnating numbers of students participating in study-away trips. Might you give us some ideas of programs that have worked for you in the past?"

[Your response—What ideas do you have to increase the number of students participating in study-away programs? How would you even define the terms "study away" or "study abroad"? Are these terms different in any way? What things need to be considered in this type of programming? How could you increase your pool of participants from minority populations and from nontraditional students?]

(IB 30/CS 62) IN-BASKET AND CASE STUDY—PROGRAM ASSESSMENT—[POLICY—COMMUNICATION—FACULTY/STAFF]

Leslie's mind was in a whirl as she entered her office. She had forgotten that an appointment with Miles Crenshaw had been scheduled; he was already waiting for her.

"Good afternoon, Dr. O'Connor."

"Oh my, Miles. I am so sorry I neglected our appointment. How late am I?"

"Twenty minutes, but that's alright."

Leslie felt flustered and stammered, "Oh, Miles, this is terrible. I always pride myself on my punctuality. It's a sign of respect . . . not that I am intentionally disrespecting you. . . ."

Miles put Leslie at ease. "Really, this is no problem, Leslie. I always bring work along with me wherever I go, in case there is some sort of delay in plans. So I have been busy reading an article."

"You're too kind, Miles. But let's go on into my office and talk about the purpose of our appointment," replied Leslie.

As the two sat down in her office, Miles continued, "As you are aware, during the recent reaffirmation visit by our regional accreditors, we were cited for not having more robust and mature academic program assessments—"

"Yes," Leslie interrupted. "We have some programs that have really stepped up to the plate, so to speak. These are doing an exceptional job in leading the way in collecting data, analyzing it, and making changes because of it. They are fantastic models of continuous quality improvement."

"That's right, Leslie. But most of our academic programs are not models. Most are adequate, at best. And, in fact, most of our nonacademic programs are barely adequate. But that's not why I've asked to speak with you."

"What is it, then, Miles?" queried Leslie.

"There are roughly six departments that are dragging their feet in completing their assessment reports, let alone carrying out any assessment procedures in the proper manner. In fact, a few of these same departments are being downright obstinate and recalcitrant. If they don't get on the same page with us soon, we will be found in noncompliance at the next evaluation. I need your help!"

> [Your response—Carry on this conversation with Dr. Crenshaw. What other questions would you have of him? What points should you emphasize? As a case study—What actions would you take in order to get the recalcitrant academic programs to take this work seriously? Whom would you plan to talk to?]

(IB 31/CS 63) IN-BASKET AND CASE STUDY—ADOPT-A-TEAM— [COMMUNICATION—NCAA—FACULTY/STUDENTS]

Leslie's next 1:1 appointment was with Athletic Director Pete Flattery. Pete had a rather assertive personality. He wasn't exactly aggressive, but he was known for being intense. He began, "Good afternoon, Ms. O'Connor. Let's get right down to it. I just got back from the conference athletic directors' meetings. One of my counterparts recently started a new program that sounds great to me, and I'd like to do something like it here at GVU."

Leslie leaned forward. Whenever she met with Pete, she felt the need to strap on a helmet—simply because of the intensity he brought to all of their conversations. "Tell me more, Pete. You have piqued my interest."

"The AD at BC has created a program she calls Adopt-a-Team. It's become a great way to help bridge the divide between the coaches and athletics side and the professors and academics side."

"What do you mean, Pete?"

Pete eagerly continued, "I don't think most of our professors understand how hard the student athletes work, the expectations placed upon them, the incredible number of hours they put in, and the fact that most of them take their studies very seriously. The idea behind Adopt-a-Team is that different academic programs would 'adopt' a specified team. For example, the English Department might adopt the women's basketball team. Or in the case of larger teams—like the football team—the Foreign Language Department might adopt the offensive line unit."

"This sounds very interesting, Pete. Tell me more about the relationship between the two. What are the faculty members' responsibilities? What expectations are placed upon them? And what is expected of the coaches and the student athletes?"

"I'm glad you asked, Leslie. Faculty members could serve as mentors, perhaps taking different players to lunch on occasion. In return, they could attend games for free. In fact, they could even travel with the team to games and be recognized at home games. They could receive free athletics gear, too. Both coaches and players would welcome these professors to games and practices, and meet with them as appropriate. None of this needs to be too formal. It's just a way for coaches, faculty members, and student athletes to better understand and appreciate each other."

> *[Your response—Continue the conversation with Pete. What other questions would you have of him? How would you proceed with creating such a program? Do you have any other ideas to help bridge the divide between academics and athletics?]*

(CS 64) CASE STUDY—HIGH-IMPACT PRACTICES—[ACADEMICS]

The end of another day was approaching. Leslie thought she would look at her email one last time before she left for the day. There was yet another email from Ben. *Didn't he promise not to write me any more emails today?* she thought.

> Leslie, I see that George Kuh will be making a speech at the state capital next month. I am a huge fan of his work on high-impact practices for student retention. He has teamed up with the American Association of Colleges and Universities to conduct a great deal of research on this topic, and I'm particularly impressed with the impact of HIPs on underrepresented populations.
> Let's meet tomorrow morning and talk about it. Visit AAC&U's website tonight to review this research. I'd like for you to attend the speech at the capital, as well. Good night.

> *[Your response—Do exactly what Ben requested. Visit the AAC&U website and investigate the research on high-impact practices, if you are not already familiar with them. Prepare for a discussion the next day with Ben on this topic.]*

Chapter Ten

Just Another Day at the Office

(CS 65) CASE STUDY—EARLY GRADUATION
WALK—[POLICY—STUDENTS]

Leslie had a phone message waiting for her as she got to work the next morning; it was from Registrar Suarez. Leslie promptly returned her call.

"Good morning, Victoria. I see that you called earlier."

Victoria pleasantly replied, "Thank you so much for returning my call, Dr. O'Connor. I have a student who is short one course to graduate. He said it was due to an advising error. When he applied to graduate, we discovered his lack of this one three-credit course requirement. It's a gen ed requirement."

"Ugh!" was all Leslie could muster.

"He said that he wants to walk at the upcoming commencement ceremony with his friends—after all, he'd been told he would be graduating then. And he says he would have taken the extra class if he had known about the situation. He did offer to take the correct class next semester if he could walk during this commencement ceremony, and that we could give him his diploma only after he successfully completed all of the course requirements."

"That sounds somewhat reasonable, Victoria. What do you think?" asked Leslie.

"I disagree. We have never allowed this sort of thing before."

"Oh, okay. Then let's deny his request," responded Leslie.

Victoria added, "There's one more thing I should mention. This student is the grandson of one of our board members."

[Your response—What would you do in this circumstance? At your own institution, review any applicable policies and talk with the appropriate staff mem-

bers. Should exceptions ever be made for friends and families of board members?]

(CS 66) CASE STUDY—STUDENT TECHNOLOGY FEE— [POLICY—COMMUNICATION—FACULTY/STUDENTS]

Leslie noticed that Ben had written her another email. It read:

> Leslie, as a reminder, I will be leaving town for the remainder of the week to attend the presidents' annual conference meetings in Florida. I'm on the planning committee, but you can reach me by phone if necessary.
>
> I have an issue that I'd like for you to resolve in the meantime. It has been brought to my attention that a number of students are complaining about the $500 annual fee for technology. They heard that it is actually used to pay for faculty development, and they don't like it. They feel their money should not be going toward this—but that the money should pay for the hardware/software that they use. It is true that roughly a third of these fees do go to faculty development. However, these funds are particularly segregated for the purpose of instructional technology training. I would like for you to write a memo to the student body in support of the need to use these funds to pay for faculty development as well.

[Your response—Do you agree with what Ben is requesting? If not, explain your reasoning and what you would write back to him. If you agree to honor this request, write the memo as he requested.]

(IB 32/CS 67) IN-BASKET AND CASE STUDY—DRUG DOGS— [POLICY—COMMUNICATION—STUDENTS]

There came a knock on her door. It was Campus Police Chief Timothy Smith.

"Good morning, Chief," Leslie began.

"Good morning, Dr. O'Connor. I have three officers from the city police department with their drug-sniffing dog out in the parking lot of Broward Hall. Late last night I received an anonymous tip that marijuana was being used in this freshmen male dormitory. So I contacted the city police to bring in their drug-sniffing dog. I stopped over to notify the vice president, but I heard he is gone for the rest of the week. So I'm just giving you a heads-up."

Leslie sat there stunned. She didn't know what to say.

[Your response—How would you continue this conversation? Script out your response and any possible answers you might receive from Chief Smith. You have four minutes to complete this task. Later, ask your mentor what policies and procedures ought to be followed for such searches. What rights do the students in the affected dormitory have, if any?]

(CS 68) CASE STUDY—FLAGGED BACKGROUND CHECK—[POLICY/LEGAL—STAFF]

As Leslie returned to her computer, the telephone rang. It was Ms. Becca Sorenson, the director of human resources.

"Dr. O'Connor, I have a bit of a dilemma for you," began the director.

"What is it, Becca?"

"As you are aware, Dean Taylor is hiring a government documents librarian, and he has a recommended final candidate."

"Sure, go on, Becca," replied Leslie.

"Of course. You are also aware that we conduct background checks on all of our position finalists. But this particular finalist has been 'red-flagged' by our service provider."

"Oh my!" Leslie exclaimed. "What for?"

"This individual has a Class D felony for driving under the influence five years ago in a different state. In addition, he did not disclose this on his employment application."

[Your response—What other questions should Leslie ask of the HR director? What is your institution's policy and protocols for background checks? Given these circumstances, should this person be hired or denied the position? Do you need any additional information to make this decision? What, in your mind, would make this hire acceptable? What would make it unacceptable?]

(IB 33/CS 69) IN-BASKET AND CASE STUDY—URGENT: VAN DRIVER NEEDED—[POLICY—COMMUNICATION]

As Leslie was wrapping up her phone conversation with Becca Sorenson, Mary walked in and handed her a note that read: "Urgent! Dean Hakeem is on hold and NEEDS to speak with you right away!"

Leslie immediately picked up the phone. "Benzar, what is it?"

"Leslie, I have an emergency. Geology Professor Viktor Mankl has taken his major students on an overnight field trip, but while they were out of town, he broke his leg and is now in the hospital."

"Oh my, Hakeem. Is he alright?"

"Yes, he is resting okay. His wife is driving up to see him."

"Okay, well, send him my best, Hakeem. And thank you for letting me know."

"Leslie, that's not the problem. The students are all still up there. They are between six and seven hours away. He was driving a school van, and he is the only person on the trip certified to drive. What should we do?"

[Your response—Continue the conversation with Dr. Hakeem. He is asking for an immediate resolution of the problem of getting these students back to campus. Finish the conversation with him right now. You have five minutes to complete this task.]

(CS 70) CASE STUDY—FAIR USE AND COPYRIGHT STANDARDS—[POLICY—ACADEMICS—COMMUNICATION—FACULTY/STUDENTS]

After dealing with these two thorny telephone calls, Leslie turned her attention back to her email. The next one to show up was from Dean Taylor of the library. The subject line read: "Fair Use and Copyright Violations."

Dr. O'Connor:
   I would like to place this item on your next deans' council meeting agenda. We have received a complaint from the bookstore staff. They are rather upset, and after learning of their concerns, I find myself in agreement with them.
   The bookstore staff have noticed that some students are not purchasing textbooks for their courses. In this particular case, after a great deal of investigating, we have found that these students are using the library to check out these same books. To make matters worse, I believe that several professors are part of this conspiracy. The evidence is that they have purchased multiple copies of these books, and they are all checked out. A number of students have gone as far as requesting an interlibrary loan for these books. Not only is this an expensive endeavor, and again, in violation of the Fair Use and Copyright Standards, but we now look like fools to our library counterparts and they likely will issue a formal complaint against us via our consortium. Finally, these same books are in the bookstore, but the number of rentals and purchases has plummeted.
   This practice must be stopped. This is a violation of the Fair Use and Copyright Standards. It is a violation of ethics for college libraries, and it is unfair to our bookstore. Please help me address this issue at the next deans' council meeting.
   Regards, Dean Taylor, LMS

[Your response—What other information would you like to obtain? Is this, indeed, a violation of the Fair Use and Copyright Standards? Does your present institution have any policies that would guide your decision on this matter? What would be your decision, and how would you enforce it?]

(CS 71) CASE STUDY—EMERITUS STAFF AND FACULTY RETIREMENT PHASEOUT—[POLICY—FACULTY/STAFF]

As Leslie began to scroll through the rest of her emails, she noticed another one from Ben. The subject line read "Two Items."

Leslie, like all universities, we have a policy on awarding emeritus standing to select faculty members upon their retirement. Recently, one of our most outstanding professional staff members announced her retirement. Someone has asked me whether it would be appropriate for us to recognize this colleague with a staff emeritus standing. Could you see if any other campuses have such a policy/practice?

In a similar vein, I attended a sectional at the conference on faculty retirement phaseouts. I'd be interested in looking into this. The idea behind this is that some faculty members would rather phase out their retirement over a couple of years, rather than face an abrupt cutoff. For example, they might reduce their teaching load by half the first year, then by three-quarters the next year, before fully retiring. Of course, this would have an impact on their benefits, and we would also want the deans' permission. With that said, since you are already going to see what other campuses are doing with regard to emeritus standing for their staff, could you also see whether they offer retirement phaseouts?

[Your response—Look to see what your institution's polices are regarding each of these ideas. This would be a perfect activity to conduct with your peers in this class.]

(CS 72) CASE STUDY—GRADE APPEAL—
[POLICY—ACADEMICS—STUDENTS/FACULTY]

This email was followed by yet another, written by Professor of Accounting Michael Nimmer, and the subject line read "Inappropriate Grade Appeal."

Dr. O'Connor:
   I wish to go on record stating my utter disdain for Dean Baong's decision to overturn my grade for Mizzi Danielson. Mizzi earned her grade of a D; in fact, I even gave her the benefit of the doubt—giving her a "mercy D." She wanted extra credit, and I don't allow that. But then she went right to the dean. He heard her sob story and overturned my grade, giving her a C–. When I asked him about this decision, he told me she couldn't graduate on time with a D, that she would have to take the course over if that was the grade she was given.
   Dr. O'Connor! That is not my concern. He does not have the right to overturn my grade. Faculty own the curriculum. We are responsible for all aspects of the curriculum, including the grading of students, and I told him so. I even went as far as telling him, "You will change that grade over my dead body." Where do you stand on this issue? I will not put up with such arbitrary and capricious intrusive behavior by administration in my domain! Good day!

Leslie got out of her chair and walked over to the window. It had been raining for some time that day, and she realized, *When it rains, it pours*. She stared out the window, considering how she would respond to Professor Nimmer.

[Your response—Of course, you will want to speak with the dean. But what questions will you ask? What points need to be considered? What does your institution's policy suggest are faculty rights and responsibilities, and what intrusions are permissible by the administration?]

(CS 73) CASE STUDY—INTELLECTUAL PROPERTY RIGHTS—[POLICY/LEGAL—ACADEMICS—FACULTY]

The final email of the day awaiting her response came from Ken Verkesne, the director of instructional technology. His subject heading read: "Intellectual Property Rights for Online Courses."

> Dear, Dr. O'Connor,
> I hope this day finds you well.
> I received an email request from a former faculty member—Beatriz Caputo. She left GVU last year to take a job at State. She developed an online course while she was here, and she taught it for two semesters. She noted that she believes that because she developed and taught the course, she owns the rights to it. With that said, she would like for me to forward to her all of the electronic documents we have stored on our server for this course, including its shell and syllabus, discussion questions, videos, assessments, and all other supplemental materials.
> My question to you is: Should I provide her all of this data? I can physically do it all—we have it all saved—but it would take me several hours to compile it and send it to her. Should I spend my time doing this? Does she, indeed, "own" the course and all of its materials?

[Your response—Precisely what are this faculty member's rights? What are the university's rights? What kinds of questions need to be asked and answered in this matter? Did she receive any course release time or faculty development funding for this work? Did she use any university resources in the development of the course? What are the intellectual property rights for faculty members as it pertains to this case? What, if anything, has the court system recently decided in these matters? Does your present institution have a policy germane to this topic?]

(IB 34/CS 74) IN-BASKET AND CASE STUDY—FACULTY VACATION—[POLICY—COMMUNICATION—FACULTY]

Leslie had finally arrived home for dinner. She'd prepared a zesty slow cooker pork chop entrée, garden salad, and baked potato covered with sour cream. She felt guilty about the latter, but she felt she deserved it after the week she had just gone through. Just as she was sipping her first glass of wine, her phone pinged. Someone had just sent a text.

She didn't recognize the number, but she read the note: "L. srry fr bthrng u at home. can i take a day uv vaca nxt fri?"

"What?" Leslie said to herself. She wrote back, "Who is this?"

"Ash Bourget. Sorry. I know faculty members don't get vacation days. But I am standing up at my sister's wedding next Saturday. I'd like Friday off to go early. Plz."

[Your response—Finish your response to Ash. You have one minute to complete your message! What would be your follow-up questions or actions, and with whom would they take place?]

Chapter Eleven

Now I've Seen Everything

(IB 35) IN-BASKET—TECHNOLOGY DOWN—
[COMMUNICATION—PLANNING]

At precisely 8:00 a.m., a message popped up on Leslie's email screen. It was from IT Director Verkesne. The subject line read "URGENT: Conferencing System Crashed!"

Dr. O'Connor:
   I left a voice message for you but am following up with this email. We are experiencing a critical problem. Our classroom video conferencing system—TechMod—is down. It has been faltering regularly, and now it is kaput. This is the system we use to link to our off-campus sites for classroom instruction. That means we presently do not have any capability to video-conference with our off-site classes, effective immediately. This is impacting roughly eight classes today, another three tonight, and another six tomorrow.
   This system is beyond antiquated. In fact, they are no longer making new systems; they are only selling old parts, and it is difficult to get them to service/install these. We could purchase some parts to fix the problem this week, but that is only a temporary solution, of course. And who knows what will happen next. If we go this route, it will cost us about $12,000. A new system would run about $80,000 and could not be installed until next semester.
   Please advise. KV

[Your response—What are you going to do? What other questions do you have for the IT director? What are some possible short-term solutions? Even the immediate solution can't be completed that day—it might take several days. What will you do in the meantime? What will you say to the students and faculty members who are relying on this technology today?]

(IB 36) IN-BASKET—TRANSGENDER ATHLETE—
[POLICY/LEGAL—NCAA]

Half an hour later, Leslie's phone rang. It was AD Flattery.

"Hey, Leslie—don't mean to interrupt you, but I need some advice. Can you help me think an issue through?"

"Sure, Pete," replied Leslie. "What is concerning you?"

"Well, you see, I heard a rumor. We have a transfer student who came here to be a cycler. As I understand it, he or she is a male, but wants to ride for the women's team. I don't know any other facts. I don't know if he's a he or he's a she. The coach doesn't know, either. This is a non-scholarship athlete whom we didn't recruit. I don't want to approach our NCAA representative with this, because I don't want to open up a can of worms. Help me think this through, please."

"This is a conundrum. It seems I read something recently about a high school transgender athlete who was a male, but who identified as a female, who won a race in a state track meet. I don't know what happened or if it is even true."

Pete responded, "Oh, it's true. I think it's still tied up in the courts."

[Your response—Continue the conversation with AD Flattery. What other questions do you have? How would you proceed?]

(CS 75) CASE STUDY—SOCIAL MEDIA ASSAULT—
[COMMUNICATION—STUDENTS]

Mary knocked urgently on Leslie's door. "I'm so sorry for interrupting, Leslie, but I have a student in crisis!"

"Please show her in, Mary," exclaimed Leslie.

A heavyset African American girl rushed into Leslie's office. She was sobbing nearly uncontrollably. But Leslie was able to make out some of her words: "They are so cruel. I hate them. They hurt me—every day!"

"What is it, honey?" was all Leslie could ask.

"Look!" With that, the girl showed Leslie her phone. On it was a screenshot of an anonymous social media post that read "Nigga bitch monique za buddha. Fat hate!"

[Your response—How do you respond in the present? What steps do you take immediately after? What rights and obligations do institutions have over social media? What are all the ramifications that must be considered and with whom do you talk?]

(CS 76) CASE STUDY—STUDENT WORKERS/WORK STUDY— [POLICY/LEGAL—STUDENTS]

Dr. Gordon stopped by to see Leslie.
"Hello, Leslie. I have to admit, I'm a bit perplexed."
"What's the problem?" Leslie replied.
"Well, I requested a work study student from HR. They wrote back to me that I can't have a 'work study' student because funding is no longer available, but I can have a 'student worker.' What does this mean? Is there a difference?"

> *[Your response—Is there a difference between "work study students" and "student workers"? If so, what is it? Who is responsible for the oversight of this area at your institution?]*

(CS 77) CASE STUDY—ADVERTISING IN STUDENT NEWSPAPER—[COMMUNICATION—POLICY]

Mary handed Leslie the day's mail. On top was a sticky note attached to the most recent issue of the student newspaper, *The Leagues*. The note read:

> Dr. O'Connor,
> Look on page 4. Our regional competitor, MSU, has a quarter-page advertisement offering summer classes at their university to our students! This just seems wrong. I don't think we should allow advertising for our competitors. R.

Leslie squinted her eyes. She wondered, *This does seem odd. And who is R?*

> *[Your response—What do you think? Is it acceptable for a competitor to advertise in your school's student newspaper? With whom should you speak? Does your institution advertise in other school newspapers?]*

(IB 37/CS 78) IN-BASKET AND CASE STUDY— SOCIAL SECURITY IDENTIFICATION— [POLICY/LEGAL—COMMUNICATION—FACULTY]

Leslie decided to walk over to the student newspaper office to speak with the editor, Aminah Busra. She had never been to their office before, and this would afford her a good opportunity to check out the operation. She and Aminah had a good conversation about the advertising policy.

As Leslie got up to leave, Aminah stopped her. "Before you leave, Dr. O'Connor, we have a student writing a guest column. He said that one of the professors posts students' midterm and final grades on the wall outside his office. Rather than identifying the students by name, he is using their Social Security numbers. Do you know anything about this?"

Leslie was stunned. "Of course not. This is an unacceptable violation!"

"A violation of what? Do you want to go on record or provide a quote for us?"

[Your response—How would you finish this conversation? What will you say? For your case study response, is this a violation? Do you have any guiding policies on this issue? Whom will you seek out for advice? How would you proceed?]

(IB 38/CS 79) IN-BASKET AND CASE STUDY—TECHNOLOGY BREACH—[POLICY/LEGAL—COMMUNICATION—PLANNING]

Irving McMaster—the vice president for informational technology—called Leslie on the telephone.

"Leslie, we have a potential crisis on our hands!" exclaimed Irving.

"What is the prob—?" Leslie began to ask.

Not waiting for her to finish, Irving continued, "I'm certain that our computer system in the student health center was hacked last night."

"Keep going, Irving," Leslie implored.

"I believe that one of our staff members accidentally left her computer on overnight. When she arrived this morning, her computer was frozen up with malware. I don't know what, if any, student records were compromised. It might be nothing, or it might be terrible," Irving responded.

"What's the worst-case scenario here?"

Irving continued, "Student health records, Social Security numbers, home addresses and phone numbers, and possibly even credit card numbers might now be in the hands of the hackers and could be shared with others!"

Leslie paused. "What should we do?" she finally asked.

"We need a computer forensic specialist to examine the office computer to see what the extent of the problem is, and if it can be determined whether or not sensitive data was stolen. And you need to communicate with the students to let them know that their data could have been breached."

[Your response—What else would you ask Irving before hanging up? Whom would you contact immediately, and what would be covered in your conversation? Talk to your supervisor at work. Who would need to be notified after a hacking incident? The law requires that people who have had their records hacked must be notified. Who would need to be notified in such a circumstance, and what should be communicated to them?]

(CS 80) CASE STUDY—CONTRACT AUTHORITY— [POLICY—COMMUNICATION]

Mary brought in a document for Leslie. "Dr. O'Connor, this is from Teresa Longstreet. It's a contract renewal for our CRM vendor. She is asking you to sign it and then mail it."

"Right, Mary. Teresa and I talked about this before with Ben. We're good to go."

"I'm not so sure, Dr. O'Connor," followed Mary.

"What do you mean?"

Mary continued, "I don't think you have the authority to sign contracts for vendors. Only the president and the vice president for administrative services are authorized to sign them."

"Oh, I'll have to check on that," replied Leslie as she took the document from Mary's hand and walked out of the office.

[Your response—At your institution, who has the authority to approve outside vendor contracts? How does the process work to obtain such approvals?]

(IB 39/CS 81) IN-BASKET AND CASE STUDY—PLAGIARISM APPEAL—[POLICY—ACADEMICS—FACULTY/STUDENTS]

A student was scheduled to meet with Leslie next. It was Arial Villereal.

"Good morning, Arial," Leslie began the conversation, motioning for the student to sit down on the chair across from her desk.

"Good morning, Dr. O'Connor. Professor Langston gave me an F for my term paper, because another student copied parts of it from me. But I didn't know she did it. She plagiarized her work from me, but I didn't give her permission to do that."

"Arial, these kinds of complaints don't come to me until all of the previous stages of appeal have been exhausted. For example, the first thing we would require is that the student talk with their professor and try to work it out by asking for a reconsideration," Leslie continued.

"I did, and Professor Langston refused," replied Arial.

"Okay, then the next step is to discuss the situation with the department chairperson, and if the issue isn't resolved satisfactorily at that level, then the student can take their appeal to the dean."

Arial seemed exasperated. "I did all of those things. Both the chair and the dean told me they would support Professor Langston because of what he had written in his syllabus."

At that point Arial showed a copy of the syllabus to Leslie. "Here it says, 'No student may wittingly or unwittingly participate in any form of plagiarism. Violation of this rule will result in an automatic F for the assignment or examination.' Dr. O'Connor, how can a student be punished for something they didn't even know happened? It's not fair!"

Leslie looked confused. "How could you not be aware of the plagiarism? What exactly happened?"

"My friend, Beth, and I always review each other's papers before we hand them in. We're in the same class. You know, we look for grammar mistakes and whether there are any better ways to write something. Well, she must have taken parts of what she read in my paper and put them in her paper. And I cited the work, but she didn't. Now I'm being punished just like her. We both got Fs. It isn't fair! How can I be punished for 'unwittingly' participating?"

Wow, she has a point, Leslie thought. Of course, she didn't say that out loud.

> [Your response—What other questions would you have for Arial? What points would you want to convey to her at this time? You have three minutes to complete this exercise. What would be your follow-up steps? With what other people would you speak, if anyone? The professor, the dean, the other student? Would you uphold the dean's decision or overturn it? On what basis?]

(PR 3) PHILOSOPHICAL REFLECTION — THE ROLE OF BUREAUCRACY AND POLICY

It was time for a special lunch with Dani Steele. Dani swung by Leslie's office bearing sub sandwiches, apples, chips, and lemonade. Sometimes a simple old-fashioned lunch was all that was needed as a break from the day-to-day hassles.

"Welcome to my humble home away from home, Dani!" Leslie began.

"This is really nice, Leslie. I like what you've done with your office," Dani noted as she looked upon the literary displays Leslie had placed on her bookshelves and in picture frames. Her diplomas were hung proudly immediately behind her desk. Indeed, it was a professional-looking office. The clutter on her desk would belie the labors of any professor of literature.

From there, the two women spent nearly a quarter of an hour talking about what they would really like to do on their summer vacations. Leslie had never been on a cruise before, and Dani regaled her with past cruise experiences to Alaska, to Europe, and to the Caribbean. They began discussing the possibility of taking a trip together the following summer.

Time was running late, but Leslie wanted some advice before Dani left. "Dani, I'm struggling a bit. I'm rather ambivalent about some of our policies. I find that I'm questioning many of them, and then I end up making decisions that I'm not comfortable with. People seem to tell me what my decision needs to be because, 'Policy says . . .'"

"I understand, Leslie," Dani interrupted. "We all have a tendency to animate policy—to personify it. Policies don't say anything. They are simply written by people to help other people make decisions."

"True, but I find myself questioning our policies more and more. Sometimes I make exceptions to them, but at other times I follow them, almost blindly. It feels like I'm flying by the seat of my pants, Dani."

"I often ask my school principals the question, 'When is a policy no longer a policy?' The answer is clear: It's when it is no longer being followed."

"But what is your point?" Leslie questioned her mentor.

"My point is that when you find you are routinely making exceptions to a policy, or even just constantly questioning it, it's time to rethink that particular policy. Perhaps the context and times surrounding it have changed. On the other hand, if it gives you leverage to make some tough decisions, then leave it alone. But there is no problem in questioning the usefulness of a policy. In fact, I believe all policies should be reviewed for this very reason somewhere between every three to five years."

"Okay, that makes sense to me. In fact, I think we could make the argument that we also need to examine our organizational structures from time to time."

"That may be true, as well, Leslie, but that would be a huge undertaking. How about you start off with analyzing just some policies first." Dani laughed.

"Of course, but I remember a term I once learned in a conference I attended. It was 'bureaupathology.' Bureaupathology exists when an organization or a bureaucracy insulates and protects itself merely for the sake of maintaining its own existence."

"I know precisely what you mean, Leslie. Such organizations make sense to those within the organization, but they make absolutely no sense to those outside of it. Hospitals and insurance companies are prime examples. But I think our school systems and universities are becoming more and more of the same. We really do need to question ourselves. I think a lot of this has been created by the legislature and by our accreditors," Dani concluded.

Leslie returned to her cookie. "Enough for now. My mind is headed back to Italy for our summer rendezvous."

[Your response—What is the purpose of policies? Give an example of a policy that seems outdated to you and needs to be updated? How would you go about making such an update? From whom would you need to seek permission? Further, examine the concept of bureaupathology. Indeed, does your own institution have any tendencies toward this problem? If so, should it be corrected, and how would you go about accomplishing that feat?]

Chapter Twelve

You Can Run, But You Can't Hide

(IB 40/CS 82) IN-BASKET AND CASE STUDY—
SPECIAL ADMISSIONS CONSIDERATION—
[POLICY/ETHICS—ACADEMICS]

Director of Undergraduate Admissions Teresa Longstreet called Leslie on the telephone. "Good afternoon, Dr. O'Connor. We have a F.O.B. request that I'd like to discuss with you."

Leslie queried, "What is an F.O.B.?"

"Oh, an F.O.B. is a 'Friend of Ben.' You see, we had a student application that did not pass muster in terms of the student's high school academic profile. In other words, the applicant is not a strong enough candidate to be accepted at GVU. However, the student is the nephew of Ben."

"Oh, hmm . . ." Leslie mumbled.

"Ben did not tell us to accept his nephew, but he did let me know that his nephew would be applying—and that while he wasn't a strong student, he'd had a good senior year and had matured. So, there was no direct request, but my staff is feeling a little pressure to accept him. Can you give me some guidance?"

[Your response—Finish the conversation with Teresa. What guidance would you give her? You have three minutes to complete this task. After Teresa leaves your office, how will you follow up on this situation?]

(CS 83) CASE STUDY—CANCELLATION POLICY FOR STUDY AWAY—[POLICY—ACADEMICS—STUDENTS]

Leslie received an email from SuYe Kim. The subject line read, "Cancellation of Study Away."

> Hello, Dr. O'Connor,
> I have a bit of a conundrum and am asking you to waive a policy. We have a junior student who had hoped to go on our J-Term trip to Rome. She is a very poor student, but I required her, like all students, to pay a $500 down payment for the trip. She did that. I also require all students to have their own insurance, or purchase our insurance, in case they cancel their reservations. She told me she was going to purchase our insurance policy but that she was having difficulty raising the funds by the deadline. I so desperately wanted her to go that I allowed her to sign up with the promise she would pay for the insurance.

Leslie rolled her eyes and said, "I don't like where I think this is going, SuYe."

> We purchased airfare, hotel, and several other itinerary-related things, for a total of $2,300. Now she can't go because she just took a part-time job; she's been homeless. So, with that said, she owes us $2,300, less the $500 down payment according to the policy. Could you please waive that and have the university "eat" the difference?
>
> *[Your response—Does your institution have a similar policy? What would it direct you to do? In this case, how would you prefer to handle this recommendation/request from your director? Are policies like this acceptable to break at times, or is a policy put in place to avoid a "slippery slope" of precedence?]*

(CS 84) CASE STUDY—R2T4—[POLICY/LEGAL—ACADEMICS—STUDENTS]

There came a knock upon Leslie's door. It was Financial Aid Director Kimberly Grasse.

"Excuse me, Dr. O'Connor, but I have a thorny issue for you. We have an R2T4 violation. A professor erroneously told a student he could withdraw from her class, but it was before the sixty percent deadline, and now we owe the federal government nearly eighteen hundred dollars. And we have these kinds of problems every year due to professors giving bad advice to students."

Leslie asked, "Is there any way we can get around this, Kimberly?"

"No, we have to pay the feds back that amount," she responded.

[Your response—What is an R2T4? What are the implications of this situation for your institution? What is the difference between "drops" and "withdrawals," and what are the implications of this difference? How can you keep this problem from happening again in the future?]

(IB 41/CS 85) IN-BASKET AND CASE STUDY—GIFT FROM VENDOR—[POLICY/ETHICS—EXTERNAL]

Leslie's lunch guest arrived right on time. Last week, Tim Graves—the regional representative of the campus bookstore—contacted Leslie to talk about some business opportunities. Today, Leslie was waiting for Tim in the outer office as he arrived.

"Welcome to Gulf Vista University, Mr. Graves," Leslie greeted him politely and tried to be welcoming.

"Oh, I've been here a hundred times before, haven't I, Mary?" Tim replied. Mary smiled and nodded her head. "Tell you what, let's get off campus today. I've got a favorite Chinese restaurant down the street. I think it's called Wok Inn."

"Sure, I know the place," Leslie demurred. With that, they headed out to the restaurant. When they arrived, Tim seemed more interested in small talk, but Leslie wanted to get down to business. She had plenty to keep her occupied. In fact, today seemed like a terrible day for an off-campus lunch, but she didn't want to cancel this meeting just to put it off into the future. Once their food arrived, they got down to business.

"So, Mr. Graves, what brings you to see me today?" Leslie began.

Dipping his spring roll into a small dish of soy sauce, he replied, "Please call me Tim. Really, Leslie, if I may, I just want to introduce myself to you and become acquainted."

"Oh, of course, Tim. I'm sorry for pressing. But I also know we're both very busy, and we appreciate your business here at Gulf Vista."

"Thank you, and I like that in you, Leslie. You're a professional dynamo. Well, you see, our company has a new opportunity we'd like to pilot with Gulf Vista University. We know how tough finals week is for all of the students. Tons of stress and demands on them. What I'd like to try with GVU is a Pride Week Giveaway. We would send emails to all of the students' parents telling them of this promo event."

"Please tell me more, Tim," came Leslie's reply.

"Well, the idea is that parents could send secret Pride Packages to their sons and daughters. They could choose one of three options—one with a baseball cap, one with a T-shirt, or one with a hoodie sweatshirt. They would pay for these online, and we would deliver them directly to the students' rooms. There is nothing that you or the university would need to do. We just need the students' parents' email addresses." He then took another swallow of his Japanese beer.

This sounded like a fun idea to Leslie, but she had so many questions.

Tim continued, "The thing is, this promotion ends today, so I need to know your answer right now. Also, as a token of our appreciation for your continued business with us, I have this Gulf Vista University Dolphins hoodie sweatshirt for you. It's the same thing we would use for the Pride Packages." With that, Tim gave Leslie a brand-new hoodie sweatshirt and signed the check to pay for the lunch.

> *[Your response—What questions do you have before you left the meeting with Mr. Graves? Would you agree to participate at that moment? You have three minutes to write out any questions you wish to ask, and write out a response to him for the moment. What are all the ramifications of making such a deal? Who needs to be a part of this decision, or does Leslie have complete authority in the decision—since the bookstore ultimately reports to her? Was it ethical for Leslie to accept the free lunch and free sweatshirt from the vendor? What does your institution's policy direct?]*

Chapter Thirteen

The End Is Near

(CS 86) CASE STUDY—CLERY ACT—[POLICY/LEGAL]

It was the weekend, and Leslie liked her routine of getting up early on Saturday mornings. She began with a forty-five-minute jog along the river. When she got home, she started her laundry and read the daily newspaper while sipping her coffee with cream. She usually followed this part of her routine with an hour of other household chores, but she was always sure to devote the time between 11:00 a.m. and noon to catch up on work-related reading. She had a similar kind of housework and "work-work" routine for the afternoon.

This morning's reading session focused on a report to the feds. Campus Police Chief Smith had given her a rough draft of the clery report, which he was responsible to write. Historically, Leslie's office had been responsible for editing it, with a particular focus on grammar, syntax, and the like. Leslie had never read a clery report before, and she was interested in reading all about it.

> *[Your response—What is the purpose of the Clery Act? What must be included in the clery report? Take this opportunity to find out who at your institution is responsible for putting this report together, then interview them and review your local report.]*

(CS 87) CASE STUDY—CONSULTING GIG—
[POLICY/ETHICS—STAFF]

Dean Baong from the School of Business sent an email to Leslie Saturday evening. The subject line read "Consulting Gig and Board Membership."

Happy Weekend, Leslie,

I hate to bother you on the weekend, and there is no rush with this item. But I do want to let you know about several opportunities that I would like to accept.

First, TopShelf Graphics would like to hire me to do some consulting work this year. They are the third largest employer in the region, and they have contributed hundreds of thousands of dollars to GVU and the School of Business over the past two decades. In any case, they would like for me to do a market analysis for them. They have offered me $15,000 to do this. Of course, I will work on this only on my own time. I just wanted to run this by you.

Second, Second Community Trust has asked me to serve a three-year term on their board of directors. This is a paid position, with a salary of $9,999 a year. I would also serve as the co-chair of their annual charity auction. Of course, with such a membership I would be expected to contribute significantly to the enterprise. This is not an uncommon practice on other campuses, however, but I wanted to run this past you, as well.

[Your response—What are the ramifications of such requests? What would your institutional policies lead you to do? From whom would you ask for advice at your campus? After considering your answers to these questions and seeking appropriate advice, write an email response back to Dean Baong.]

Chapter Fourteen

Don't Count Your Eggs Before They're Hatched

(IB 42/CS 88) IN-BASKET AND CASE STUDY—FACULTY ROLE IN ADMISSIONS STANDARDS—[POLICY—FACULTY]

Monday morning's first appointment for Leslie was with Faculty Senate President Bouche. After the usual pleasantries were exchanged, Barbara got to the point, in a friendly manner.

"Leslie, I've expressed concern to you from the faculty about an apparent trend in the academic qualifications of our students—they seem to be less and less prepared each year."

"Yes, anecdotally that feeling has been shared, Barbara. But the statistics show this isn't the case. In fact, the academic profile is improving. ACT and SAT scores are improving, as are high school GPAs of incoming students."

"Well, the GPAs are basically meaningless with grade inflation these days. Nevertheless, the faculty senate has asked me to talk with you. They would like to place a faculty representative on the admissions committee to be part of their decision-making process. AAU&P tells us that historically admissions standards fall under the purview of the faculty."

> *[Your response—How would you finish this conversation with the faculty senate president? Would you promise to allow for faculty representation? Do you have other questions for the faculty senate presdent? Consider the membership of your institution's admissions committee. Who makes the decisions? How do they arrive at these decisions? In other words, what criteria do they follow, and do they allow for any flexibility? Does the faculty have any role in the decision-making process? After you consider these questions, draft an email response to the faculty senate president.]*

(CS 89) CASE STUDY—STUDENT NEWSPAPER QUOTE—[COMMUNICATION—STUDENTS]

Leslie decided to get out of the office for a break. She walked across the quad to the library and thought she'd sit down on a comfortable chair overlooking the beautiful courtyard. She grabbed the most recent issue of the student newspaper. The lead article's headline, stretched across the bottom half of the front page, read "AVP O'Connor Admonishes Faculty."

Quickly, Leslie read the article. It focused on the professor whom Aminah had discussed with her just in the past week. The professor was named—Dr. Langston. The article included quotes from various students complaining about their Social Security numbers and grades being posted on the wall outside of the professor's office. A quote from Leslie was also embedded in a sentence; it read, "Dr. O'Connor reacted, 'This is a violation and is unacceptable.'"

Leslie was beside herself, and she felt her ears turning read. She thought, *I did say that, but I told her not to quote me!*

At that moment her cell phone rang. It was Mary. She told Leslie, "Dr. O'Connor, President Boggs stopped by. He told me that he would like to see you."

"I'll be right there, Mary." With that, Leslie made a beeline across the quad.

[Your response—What will you convey to Dr. Boggs about the article? What will you convey to Aminah? Will you write a response to the article? Why or why not?]

(IB 43/CS 90) IN-BASKET AND CASE STUDY—TOGA, TOGA, TOGA!—[POLICY—COMMUNICATION—STUDENTS]

After calmly listening to President Boggs's concerns about her quote in the newspaper, coupled with the issue of a faculty member posting students' Social Security numbers, Leslie briefly shared her side of the story. She then returned to her office, only to see a student waiting for her. It was not someone she recognized.

The young man stood and introduced himself. "Hello, Dr. O'Connor. I'm Drew Rutledge, and I serve as the local chapter president of Alpha Omega Beta."

"Oh, it's nice to meet you, Drew. What can I do for you?" Leslie inquired, still a bit upset after her verbal exchange with the university president.

"The dean of students—Dr. Korschvitz—said I needed to see you. You see, my fraternity had a toga party this past weekend. Apparently a few pledges brought in some alcohol. They were underage, and the campus police arrested them. Our chapter and national bylaws tell us how to respond to such incidents, and we plan to adjudicate this issue and sanction those involved. But the dean wants to adjudicate this incident himself through Student Affairs. We don't feel this is fair, because we will be punishing these recalcitrant underclassmen, too. In fact, I'm sure our punishment will actually be quite harsher."

"Okay, Drew, let's sit down and discuss this."

[Your response—What questions do you have for Drew at this time? What points do you need to convey to him before he leaves your office? What policies and protocols does your institution have in place for such situations? What are the issues to be addressed with Student Affairs, with the fraternity, and with the campus police? How would you handle this complex situation?]

(CS 91) CASE STUDY—RFP—[POLICY/LEGAL]

Ben stopped Leslie in the hallway and told her he thought GVU's work-flow processes might be outdated; certainly, he thought, they needed a review. Over time, it seemed that because so many steps had been added to processes, the full picture had become obscured. New technology only exacerbated and highlighted these concerns. Ben wanted Leslie to find someone from outside of the university to give it a look with a fresh set of eyes.

Leslie had just the person in mind: a colleague from her former institution who had done similar consulting work in the past. She walked over to the office of the vice president for administration and finance, Hector Contreras, to ask how to approach her former colleague to contract his services.

After she told Hector the scope of what she needed, he said, "We can't just hire a consultant for such a task. We need to put out an RFP."

"What? Why? I'm estimating this will only cost less than $2,500 over one month's time."

"Sure. But let's still put out an RFP," Hector responded.

[Your response—At what point does your institution require an RFP for outside services? What is involved in putting together an RFP at your institution?]

(CS 92) CASE STUDY—BUDGET CUTS—[COMMUNICATION—ACADEMICS]

Leslie received an email from Ben. The subject line read "Budget Cuts—Grad Assistants."

Leslie,

98   Chapter 14

At this morning's senior staff meeting, we created a framework for 10 percent budget cuts for the university. The cuts are expected to be from the remainder of the fiscal year and are precautionary. In other words, these cuts may or may not go into effect, but we want to be prepared. These potential cuts will not be across the board. Some programs will not be cut at all; some programs or departments may have to cut as much as 15 percent. Impact on instruction will be kept to a minimum.

The senior staff has decided that we will cut the graduate assistants positions by 15 percent. By the end of the week, I will need to see your plan on how these cuts will be implemented.

Enjoy. Ben

[Your response—What questions would you like to ask Ben regarding this email? How would you go about making the cuts he has requested? What process would you use to make these decisions? What information do you need? Will anyone else help you to make such decisions? If so, what will be the level of their involvement? Will you make an argument in favor of saving some of these positions? If so, what would be the argument?]

(IB 44) IN-BASKET—CAN YOU DO ME A FAVOR?—[ETHICS—COMMUNICATION]

Leslie sat back in her chair. This was going to be an unpleasant task, but she had gone through budget cut exercises before. Just then her phone rang. It was her mentor, Dr. Dani Steele.

"Good afternoon, Dani! How are you doing?" Leslie began.

"I'm well, Leslie. I'm doing quite well. What about yourself?"

"As my dad used to say, 'Fair to middlin','" was all Leslie could muster. "To what do I owe the pleasure of your call?"

"Well, my niece just graduated from Upstate with her bachelor's degree in psychology. She is looking to return home now," replied Dani.

"Congratulations! You should be very proud."

Dani continued, "Indeed, we are. And that brings me to the purpose of my call, besides just checking in to see how you are faring. She is looking for a job, and we noticed a posting at an admissions office recruiter."

Leslie simply replied with, "Mmm-hmm."

"I'm not asking any untoward favors, of course, Leslie. But could you see that she gets interviewed for the job? I'm not asking for her to be given the job, just to get an interview," Dani explained.

[Your response—How would you finish this phone call with your mentor? Would you have any other questions for her? What promises could you realistically make? Depending on your response, what would you say to the director of the undergraduate admissions office?]

(CS 93) CASE STUDY—FACULTY SENATE VOTE— [SHARED GOVERNANCE—POLICY—COMMUNICATION]

Leslie returned to her email. She saw the typical reminder in her in-box of the upcoming faculty senate meeting from Senate Chair Barbara Bouche. She printed off the attached agenda and minutes from the previous month's meeting, then began to read both documents. Something immediately caught her eye. On the agenda, under "New Business," she saw the item "Online Teaching Referendum."

What is this about? Leslie thought. *Our university president has been fundamentally opposed to fully online academic programs. He did, however, accept the notion of hybrid and online courses. In fact, he recently spoke publicly about the need to expand our online offerings. Is this agenda item a reaction to that issue?*

> *[Your response—Would you wait until the meeting to hear what this agenda item is actually about? Or would you begin to dig a little to determine what the issue is about? If so, with whom would you speak and what would you ask?]*

(CS 94) CASE STUDY—BAD STUDENT EVALUATIONS— [POLICY—COMMUNICATION—FACULTY/STUDENTS]

One part of the job that Leslie had always taken very seriously—and sensitively—was the faculty evaluative feedback from students. Today, she received an electronic report of all of the evaluations for each faculty member, organized by course, including those taught by adjuncts.

As she reviewed each of the files one by one, she took notes of issues to discuss with the individual deans. Most particularly, she was looking for outlier ratings or pertinent comments by students. She was reminded of a quote by a former colleague: "If one person calls you a horse's hindquarters, you ignore it; if two people call you a horse's hindquarters, you perk up your ears; if three people call you a horse's hindquarters, you put on a saddle." She made special notes where such themes emerged.

While she ended up writing notes on roughly ten instructors, Leslie was amazed at how positive and affirming the student feedback actually was. Of course, certain courses had more than the average lower ratings. These courses were in the math and sciences department, but nothing too bad was recorded. However, two instructors—one tenured faculty member and one adjunct instructor—had surprisingly consistent negative ratings and comments.

On a four-point rating scale, the professor averaged 2.2. Comments varied from, "This professor is arrogant and has class favorites," to "He is extremely rude and condescending." Other comments stated, "Doesn't keep office hours," to "Cancels class without telling us ahead of time."

The adjunct instructor had even worse ratings, 1.7 on average, and the feedback from the comments was terrible. Such feedback included: "Worst professor I have ever had," to "Doesn't know what he is talking about." Other comments included, "Very unorganized and unprepared for class," to "Lectures from the book," and "The tests don't match what is taught in class." Leslie's notepad was full. She was going to meet with the appropriate deans to discuss a plan of action for each of these two teachers.

[Your response—How would you handle such feedback? Would you let the deans take care of the situation, or would you get involved yourself? If you were like Leslie and wanted to speak with the deans, what would you say? Would you recommend that these instructors be put on some sort of action plan? Would you speak to them personally? Would you implement a follow-up process? Would you handle the tenured faculty member differently than the adjunct instructor?]

References

American Association of University Professors. (1966). *Statement on Government of Colleges and Universities.* Washington, DC: aaup.org/report/statement-government-colleges-and-universities.

Bowen, W., and Tobin, E. (2015). *Locus of Authority: The Evolution of Faculty Roles in the Governance of Higher Education.* Princeton, NJ: Princeton University Press.

Delaware Cost Study: www.ire.udel.edu/cost; www.ire.udel.edu/descriptive-summary/.

Goleman, D. (March 2000). "Leadership That Gets Results," *Harvard Business Review,* 78–90.

Hersey, P., and Blanchard, K. (1988). *Management of Organizational Behavior: Utilizing Human Resources.* 6th ed. Upper Saddle River, NJ: Prentice Hall.

High Impact Practices: www.aacu.org/resources/high-impact-practices.

Kotter, J. (1999). *What Leaders Really Do.* Cambridge, MA: Harvard Business School Press.

Lounder, A. (2016). *Shared Governance: Is OK Good Enough?* Washington, DC: Association of Governing Boards of Universities and Colleges.

McGregor, D. (1960). *The Human Side of Enterprise.* New York: McGraw-Hill.

National Student Clearinghouse: www.studentclearinghouse.org.

Responsibility-Centered Management: www.indiana.edu/~obap/rcm-iub.php.

Rettig, P. (2004). *Practicing Principals: Case Studies, In-Baskets, and Policy Analysis.* Lanham, MD: Rowman & Littlefield.

Index of Cases, In-Baskets, and Professional Reflections

The Interview	4–12
Preparation	2, 4
Questions and Answers	
IB 1—Comfort Dog—[Policy—Students]	13
IB 2—Vacation Request—[Policy—Staff]	14
IB 3—Family on Study Away—[Policy—Faculty/Staff]	14
IB 4—Confidential—[Ethics]	14
IB 5—Black Student Union—[Policy—Students]	14
CS 1—In-Depth Review	15
CS 2—Strategic Planning—[Planning]	15
IB 6—Phone Call—Student Newspaper—[Communication]	16
IB 7—Walk-In Visitor—Faculty Senate—[Communication]	16
IB 8—Study Away—Change in Plans—[Policy]	16
IB 9—Phone Call—Collaborative Partnership—[Communication—External]	17
IB 10—Enrollment Management—[Communication]	18
CS 3—In-Depth Review	18
CS 4—Pay for Play?—[NCAA]	18
CS 5—Need for Tenure?—[Faculty]	19

CS 6—Prayer Request—[Policy—Students]	21
CS 7—Muslim Safe Place—[Policy—Communication—Students]	22
IB 11—Undocumented Students—[Policy—Students]	22
CS 8—Active Shooter: Tabletop—[Policy—Communication]	23
IB 12/CS 9—Property Rights—[Communication—Students]	23
CS 10—Dashboards—[Planning—Communication]	24
IB 13—Alcohol Violation—[Policy—Ethics—Faculty]	24
IB 14—Admissions Tours—[Communication—Students]	25
CS 11—Freedom of Speech—[Policy—Communication]	25
IB 15—Staff Meeting Agenda—[Planning]	26
CS 12—New Academic Program—[Policy—Academics]	27
IB 16—Walkabout—[Communication]	27
IB 17—Transcript Hold—[Policy—Students]	28
IB 18—Parent Concern/FERPA—[External—Communication (Student/Faculty)]	28
CS 13—Athletes' Special Treatment—[NCAA]	29
CS 14—Personal Politics in Class—[Policy—Communication—Faculty]	29
CS 15—Confederate Flag—[Policy—Ethics—Communication]	30
CS 16—Sidewalk Chalk—[Policy—Students]	31
CS 17—Enrollment Data Sharing—[Policy—Communication]	31
CS 18—Tutoring Help—[Policy—Staff]	32
CS 19—Outside Work—[Policy—Faculty]	32
IB 19—Care Packages—[Policy—External]	33
CS 20—KIT/IPEDS—[Policy—Planning and Data Management]	33
CS 21—IRB—[Policy—Faculty]	34
CS 22—Intellectual Property—[Policy—Ethics—Faculty]	34
IB 20—Foreign Student in Dorms—[Policy—Students]	35
IB 21—Alumni Opportunity—[Communication—External]	35
CS 23—Adjunct Pay—[Policy—Faculty]	36
IB 22/CS 24—Academic Integrity—[Policy—Students]	36

Index of Cases, In-Baskets, and Professional Reflections

CS 25—Academic Program Review—[Policy—Academics]	37
IB 23—Overruled—[Communication]	37
IB 24—Grade Appeal/Bell Curve—[Policy—Faculty/Students]	38
CS 26—Financial Aid Disclosure/Beauty School Dropout—[Policy—Students]	38
CS 27—Professional Development—[Policy—Faculty]	41
CS 28—Assault—[Policy—Students]	42
CS 29—Hazing—[Policy—Communication—Students]	42
CS 30—Social Media—[Communication—Policy—Staff]	43
CS 31—Budget Request—[Communication—Policy]	43
CS 32—Student Course Evaluations—[Policy—Communication—Faculty/Students]	44
CS 33—Transgender Student—[Policy/Ethics—Students]	44
CS 34—Sunsetting Programs—[Policy—Academics]	45
CS 35—Average Class Size—[Policy—Academics]	45
CS 36—Leadership Philosophy—[Communication]	46
CS 37—Search and Screen—[Policy—Staff]	46
CS 38—Diversity in the Classroom—[Policy—Communication—Faculty/Staff]	47
CS 39—Student Course Evaluations—[Policy—Faculty/Students]	48
CS 40—Low-Enrolled Programs—[Policy—Academics]	48
IB 25—Faculty Dishonesty—Fraudulent Syllabus—[Policy—Ethics—Faculty]	49
CS 41—Advancement Fund-Raiser—[Communication—External]	49
IB 26—Dean Argument—Tempers—[Communication—Staff]	51
CS 42—Facebook Request—[Communication—Ethics—Students]	52
CS 43—Anonymous Complaint—[Ethics—Communication—Staff]	52
CS 44—Special Treatment for Athletes—[NCAA]	52
CS 45—Kente Stole—[Communication—Policy—Students]	53

IB 27—Social Media in the Workplace—[Communication—Ethics/Policy—Students/Staff]	54
CS 46—Starting a New Student Organization—[Policy—Students]	54
CS 47—Online Instruction—[Policy—Academics—Communication]	55
CS 48—O Christmas Tree—[Policy—Communication—Staff]	56
CS 49—Staff Council—[Policy—Communication—Staff]	57
PR 1—Philosophical Reflection—[Power and Authority]	57
CS 50—Split Vote on Tenure—[Policy—Faculty]	61
CS 51—Tutoring Lowers Grades?—[Policy/Ethics—Communication—Faculty]	62
IB 28/CS 52—Changing Tradition/Symbols—[Communication]	63
IB 29—Default Rate—[Policy—Academics—Communication]	64
CS 53—Letter of Reprimand—[Policy/Ethics—Communication—Staff]	64
CS 54—National Clearinghouse—[Policy—Academics—Communication]	65
CS 55—Pell Grants—[Policy—Academics—Communication]	65
CS 56—Instructional Technology Platform—[Academics]	65
CS 57—Nontraditional Students—[Planning—Students]	66
PR 2—Philosophical Reflection—[Motivation Principles]	66
CS 58—Summer Bridge—[Academics—Students]	67
CS 59—Administrator Performance Reviews—[Policy—Staff]	68
CS 60—Responsibility-Centered Management—[Policy—Planning]	68
CS 61—Study Away—[Academics—Students]	69
IB 30/CS 62—Program Assessment—[Policy—Communication—Faculty/Staff]	69
IB 31/CS 63—Adopt-a-Team—[Communication—NCAA—Faculty/Students]	70
CS 64—High-Impact Practices—[Academics]	71
CS 65—Early Graduation Walk—[Policy—Students]	73

CS 66—Student Technology Fee—[Policy—Communication— 74
Faculty/Students]

IB 32/CS 67—Drug Dogs—[Policy—Communication— 74
Students]

CS 68—Flagged Background Check—[Policy/Legal—Staff] 75

IB 33/CS 69—Urgent: Van Driver Needed—[Policy— 75
Communication]

CS 70—Fair Use and Copyright Standards—[Policy— 76
Academics—Communication—Faculty/Students]

CS 71—Emeritus Staff and Faculty Retirement Phaseout— 77
[Policy—Faculty/Staff]

CS 72—Grade Appeal—[Policy—Academics—Students/ 77
Faculty]

CS 73—Intellectual Property Rights—[Policy/Legal— 78
Academics—Faculty]

IB 34/CS 74—Faculty Vacation—[Policy—Communication— 79
Faculty]

IB 35—Technology Down—[Communication—Planning] 81

IB 36—Transgender Athlete—[Policy/Legal—NCAA] 82

CS 75—Social Media Assault—[Communication—Students] 82

CS 76—Student Workers/Work Study—[Policy/Legal— 83
Students]

CS 77—Advertising in Student Newspaper— 83
[Communication—Policy]

IB 37/CS 78—Social Security Identification—[Policy/Legal— 83
Communication—Faculty]

IB 38/CS 79—Technology Breach—[Policy/Legal— 84
Communication—Planning]

CS 80—Contract Authority—[Policy—Communication] 85

IB 39/CS 81—Plagiarism Appeal—[Policy—Academics— 85
Faculty/Students]

PR 3—Philosophical Reflection—[The Role of Bureaucracy 86
and Policy]

IB 40/CS 82—Special Admissions Consideration—[Policy/ 89
Ethics—Academics]

CS 83—Cancellation Policy for Study Away—[Policy—Academics—Students]	90
CS 84—R2T4—[Policy/Legal—Academics—Students]	90
IB 41/CS 85—Gift from Vendor—[Policy/Ethics—External]	91
CS 86—Clery Act—[Policy/Legal]	93
CS 87—Consulting Gig—[Policy/Ethics—Staff]	93
IB 42/CS 88—Faculty Role in Admissions Standards—[Policy—Faculty]	95
CS 89—Student Newspaper Quote—[Communication—Students]	96
IB 43/CS 90—Toga, Toga, Toga!—[Policy—Communication—Students]	96
CS 91—RFP—[Policy/Legal]	97
CS 92—Budget Cuts—[Communication—Academics]	97
IB 44—Can You Do Me a Favor?—[Ethics—Communication]	98
CS 93—Faculty Senate Vote—[Shared Governance—Policy—Communication]	99
CS 94—Bad Student Evaluations—[Policy—Communication—Faculty/Students]	99

About the Author

Perry R. Rettig, PhD, has published four books with Rowman & Littlefield. A former public school principal and teacher, he has written extensively on myriad educational leadership topics. In his fifth year as vice president for academic affairs at Piedmont College and as a professor of educational leadership for the past twenty years, he has turned his research focus to higher educational leadership. Pragmatic preparation for preservice university administrators and a particular emphasis on the principles of shared governance provide his current scholarship.

www.ingramcontent.com/pod-product-compliance
Lightning Source LLC
Chambersburg PA
CBHW020750230426
43665CB00009B/561